A Woman's Dilemma
Mercy Otis Warren
and the
American Revolution

Rosemarie Zagarri
George Mason University

Harlan Davidson, Inc.
Wheeling, Illinois 60090-6000

Library of Congress Cataloging-in-Publication Data

Zagarri, Rosemarie, 1957–
    A woman's dilemma : Mercy Otis Warren and the
American revolution / Rosemarie Zagarri
        p. cm. — (American biographical history series)
    Includes bibliographical references (p. 168) and index.
    ISBN 0-88295-924-7
    1. Warren, Mercy Otis, 1728–1814. 2. United States—
History—Revolution, 1775–1783—Women. 3. Women
authors, American—18th century—Biography. 4. Women
historians—United States—Biography.
    I. Title. II. Series.
PS858.W8Z97   1995
973.3'092—dc20
    [B]   94-38205
                                         CIP

Cover detail from frontispiece: Bequest of Winslow Warren,
Courtesy, Museum of Fine Arts, Boston

Manufactured in the United States of America
98   97   96   95   1   2   3   4   5   MG

To Anthony

CONTENTS

As biographies offer access to the past, they reflect the needs of the present. Newcomers to biography and biographical history often puzzle over the plethora of books that some lives inspire. "Why do we need so many biographies of Abraham Lincoln?" they ask, as they search for the "correct" version of the sixteenth president's story. Each generation needs to revisit Lincoln because each generation has fresh questions, inspired by its own experiences. Collectively, the answers to these questions expand our understanding of Lincoln and America in the 1860s, but they also assist us to better comprehend our own time. People concerned with preserving such civil liberties as freedom of the press in time of national crisis have looked at Lincoln's approach to political opposition during and after secession. Civil rights activists concerned with racial injustice have turned to Lincoln's life to clarify unresolved social conflicts that persist more than a century after his assassination.

Useful as it is to revisit such lives, it is equally valuable to explore those often neglected by biographers. Almost always, biographies are written about prominent individuals who changed, in some measure, the world around them. But who is prominent and what constitutes noteworthy change are matters of debate. Historical beauty is definitely in the eye of the beholder. That most American biographies tell of great white males and their untainted accomplishments speaks volumes about the society that produced such uncritical paeans. More recently, women and men of various racial, religious, and economic backgrounds have expanded the range of American biography. The lives of prominent African-American leaders, Native American chieftains, and immigrant sweatshop workers who climbed the success ladder to its top now crowd onto those library shelves next to familiar figures.

In the American Biographical History Series, specialists in key areas of American History describe the lives of important men and women of many different races, religions, and ethnic backgrounds as those figures shaped and were shaped by the political, social, economic, and cultural issues of their day and the people with whom they lived. Biographical subjects and readers share a dialogue across time and space as biographers pose the questions suggested by life in modern-day America to those who lived in other eras. Each life offers a timeless reservoir of answers to questions from the present. The result is at once edifying and entertaining.

The concise biographical portrait found in each volume in this series is enriched and made especially instructive by the attention paid to generational context. Each biographer has taken pains to link his or her subject to peers and predecessors engaged in the same area of accomplishment. Even the rare individuals whose ideas or behavior transcend their age operated within a broad social context of values, attitudes, and beliefs. Iconoclastic radicals, too, whatever their era, owed a debt to earlier generations of protesters and left a legacy for those who would resist the status quo in the future.

Biographers in the series offer readers new companions, individuals of accomplishment, whose lives and works can be weighed and assessed and consulted as resources in answering the nagging questions that the thoughtful in every generation ask of the past to better comprehend the present. The makers of America—male and female, black and white and red and yellow, Christian, Moslem, Jew, atheist, agnostic, and polytheist, rich and poor and in between—all testify with their lives that the past is prologue. Anxious to share his rich experiences with those willing to listen, an elderly Eastern European immigrant living in Pittsburgh boasted, "By myself, I'm a book!" He, too, realized that an important past could be explicated through the narrative of a life, in fact, his own.

When a biographer sees his or her subject in broader context, important themes are crystallized, an era is illuminated. The single life becomes a window to a past age and its truths for succeeding generations and for you.

ALAN M. KRAUT
JON L. WAKELYN

Mrs. James Warren (Mercy Otis), about 1763
Courtesy, Museum of Fine Arts, Boston

ACKNOWLEDGMENTS

Just as Mercy Otis Warren's *History of the American Revolution* owed its existence to the intervention and assistance of numerous friends and acquaintances, so, too, does this biography of its author. Reaching very far back, I would like to acknowledge the influence of four teachers, Sr. Marie Blanche Marschner, S.S.N.D., Sr. Miriam Catherine Wesselman, S.S.N.D., Sr. Sheila Marie Hederman, C.S.J., and Ms. Mary Jo Mason, all of whom demonstrated in their lives and classrooms that gender was no barrier to intellectual equality. My graduate school mentor provided another kind of assistance. I owe my title to Edmund S. Morgan's *The Puritan Dilemma: The Story of John Winthrop*, which remains a model and inspiration for all biographers.

More immediately, several people contributed to the origin and development of this project. Jon Wakelyn, my colleague and friend, proved to be a superb editor. He encouraged the idea from the start and nudged its skittish author toward the work's completion. Alan Kraut, coeditor of the American Biographical History Series, did yeoman service in providing helpful editorial comments and gentle recommendations for revision. The Charles Pyne Family of Sandwich, Massachusetts, kindly offered me a place to stay as I searched out Mercy's homes in the region. Alexa Crane of the Sturgis Library in Barnstable aided me in locating the site of the Otis family home. Although the house has been destroyed, a stone marker in honor of James Otis near the intersection of Massachusetts Route 6A and Highway 149 provides a clue as to the location.

Other colleagues and friends have read the manuscript closely and made perceptive suggestions for its improvement. I especially thank Edie Gelles, Ann Hulbert, Laura Kalman, Sheila Skemp, and Barbara Clark Smith who took time from their own demanding schedules to perform this service for me. Kim Gray, Robin Chapman Stacey, Ellen Warnock-Eckhart, Larry Poos, and Anthony V. Z. Morley did little to contribute to the project directly. They did, however, have the all-important task of keeping up the biographer's spirits. For "banter[ing] and laugh[ing] me out of [my] whimsical Gloom," as James Warren did for Mercy, I thank them.

The Massachusetts Historical Society in Boston has kindly granted me permission to quote from the Mercy Warren papers. For the convenience of scholars, I have deposited there a list of references to the quotations used within this book. Interested parties may obtain a copy of the citations from the Society. All quotations have been rendered as written in the original documents, complete with the irregular spellings and punctuation common at the time.

Rosemarie Zagarri

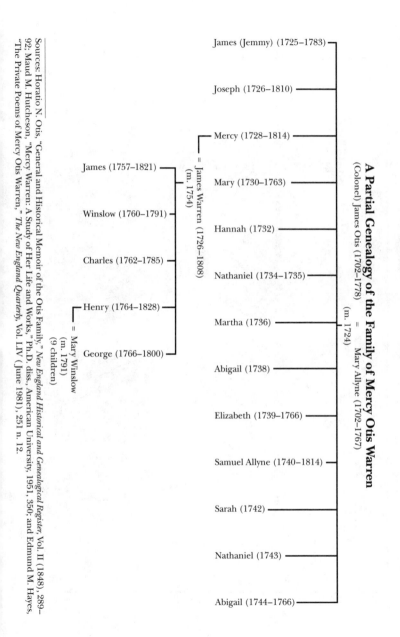

A Partial Genealogy of the Family of Mercy Otis Warren

(Colonel) James Otis (1702–1778)
=
Mary Allyne (1702–1767)
(m. 1724)

James (Jemmy) (1725–1783)

Joseph (1726–1810)

Mercy (1728–1814)
=
James Warren (1726–1808)
(m. 1754)

James (1757–1821)

Winslow (1760–1791)

Charles (1762–1785)

Henry (1764–1828)
=
Mary Winslow
(m. 1791)
(9 children)

George (1766–1800)

Mary (1730–1763)

Hannah (1732)

Nathaniel (1734–1735)

Martha (1736)

Abigail (1738)

Elizabeth (1739–1766)

Samuel Allyne (1740–1814)

Sarah (1742)

Nathaniel (1743)

Abigail (1744–1766)

Sources: Horatio N. Otis, "General and Historical Memoir of the Otis Family," *New England Historical and Genealogical Register,* Vol. II (1848), 289–92; Maud M. Hutcheson, "Mercy Warren: A Study of Her Life and Works," Ph.D. diss., American University, 1951, 350; and Edmund M. Hayes, "The Private Poems of Mercy Otis Warren," *The New England Quarterly,* Vol. LIV (June 1981), 251 n. 12.

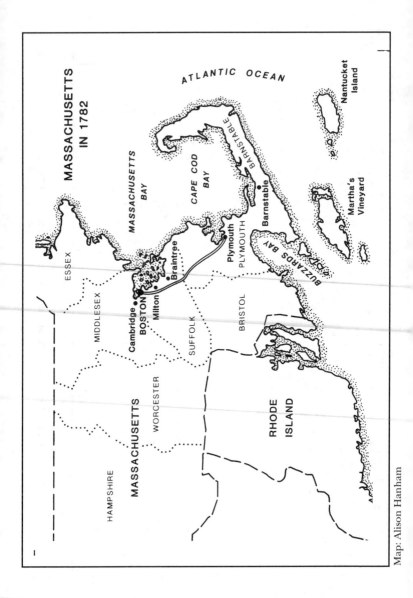

MASSACHUSETTS IN 1782

ATLANTIC OCEAN

Nantucket Island

Martha's Vineyard

MASSACHUSETTS BAY

CAPE COD BAY

BARNSTABLE

Barnstable

BUZZARDS BAY

Plymouth

PLYMOUTH

ESSEX

MIDDLESEX

Cambridge
BOSTON
Milton
Braintree

SUFFOLK

BRISTOL

RHODE ISLAND

MASSACHUSETTS

HAMPSHIRE

WORCESTER

Map: Alison Hanham

INTRODUCTION

In the pantheon of famous American women, figures such as Abigail Adams and Betsy Ross have often received considerable attention. Yet few people outside the world of academe have heard of the women's more accomplished contemporary, Mercy Otis Warren. Based solely on the record of their respective achievements, it is Warren who is the more deserving of recognition. Reviewing Warren's career, a personage no less than Thomas Jefferson commented on her "high station in the ranks of genius." John Adams regarded her, along with his wife, as "the most accomplished Lady in America." Considering her work, Alexander Hamilton remarked that "in the career of dramatic compositions at least, female genius has outstripped the Male." Judith Sargent Murray, an aspiring female author herself, saw in Warren a role model: "the literary Votaress, aspiring to distinction, will ambitiously seek to authorize her pretensions by the Celebrious name of Warren."

Mercy Otis Warren gained recognition on her own merits, not only through her relationships with famous men. She was a writer and a political thinker, a correspondent—some might even say consultant—to political leaders such as John Adams, George Washington, Elbridge Gerry, and others. She produced several caustic political satires lampooning British tyranny in the 1770s, authored an incisive tract opposing the ratification of the U.S. Constitution in 1788, issued a volume of selected poems and plays in 1790, and in 1805 published one of the earliest histories of the American Revolution. Although she initially published her writings anonymously, she eventually became the first American woman to publish political works under her own name.

Nor was she a recluse as she penned these works. As the wife of one patriot and the sister of another, she ran a comfortable, well-ordered household that became a salon for revolutionaries. She was the proud mother of five sons. At the center of a network of female friends, she corresponded with well-known women such as Abigail Adams and the British historian Catharine Macaulay, as well as with a variety of lesser-known friends, acquaintances, and family members. Her long life lasted from 1728, when Massachusetts was still a British colony, until 1814, when the United States, now an independent nation, was again at war with Great Britain.

To the modern reader, the life of Mercy Otis Warren may pose a paradox. Though confident of her literary and intellectual abilities, she depended on men, especially John Adams, to give her a special dispensation to write about "male" political matters. Though certain of the intellectual equality of the sexes, she believed in the "appointed subordination (perhaps for the sake of order in families)" of women to men. Though a productive author, she insisted that women must put their domestic, wifely, and motherly duties ahead of intellectual endeavors. With proper household management, she insisted, writing could be squeezed into the interstices of the busy day's regularly occupied time. As immersed as she was in politics, she led no drive for women's suffrage. When Abigail Adams indignantly reported to Warren that her husband had dismissed her plea to "Remember the Ladies" when writing the Massachusetts state constitution, Warren responded with silence. Though she chafed at "the narrow bounds, prescrib'd to female life," as she put it in one of her poems, Mercy accepted without question the existing gender status quo.

Eventually, however, the contradictions in her position came to haunt her. Toward the end of her career, in a sad denouement to their friendship, Mercy and her former mentor, John

Adams, engaged in a bitter fight over the purportedly unflattering portrayal of him in her *History of the American Revolution.* Once Mercy's pen had been turned on him, Adams dismissed her work, saying, "History is not the Province of the Ladies." In an extended exchange of letters, Mercy defended herself as best she could against Adams's invectives; but the powerlessness of her position was evident. She had no explicit justification for her behavior. Her credibility ultimately rested on men's willingness to tolerate her encroachment into their territory. Warren was thus a woman of singular distinction—but also singularly vulnerable for having violated existing gender norms.

Mercy Otis Warren's life offers a fascinating perspective on the American Revolution. Like many other colonists, male and female alike, she moved within a relatively short time from unquestioned support for the mother country, to loyal opposition, to outright rebellion. As the author of political tracts, she became a propagandist against Britain, a critic of the U.S. Constitution, and a staunch Democratic-Republican. Voicing classical republican ideas, she consistently maintained that republican government depended on the virtue of the citizens. For most of her life, she found herself a member of the opposition, and she used her pen as her weapon.

Yet Mercy's life offers more than the typical example of one patriot's journey. Unlike her male counterparts, she had to overcome her sex in order to become a patriot. As a woman, she was neither expected to join nor automatically welcomed into the resistance movement. But she persisted and made an important, unique contribution. In the end, her career reveals both the limits and possibilities of woman's role in revolutionary America. Mercy showed what a smart, educated woman could accomplish with the necessary encouragement and ambition; but she also discovered that without an articulated rationale to explain her behavior—without an ideology of feminism—she constantly felt ill at ease about her activities.

She was frequently open to attacks, both real and imagined, for having violated her assigned sphere. Her life thus demonstrates how an exceptional woman could manipulate existing gender roles with great success, but also how constricting those roles could ultimately be. Warren's struggle, then, represented not just a battle against Great Britain, but a struggle against the limits of womanhood itself.

CHAPTER ONE

The First Friends of Her Heart

Fourteen-year-old Mercy Otis had dreamed for months about her brother James's upcoming graduation from Harvard. Never before had she ventured more than a few miles from her childhood home in the Cape Cod town of Barnstable, Massachusetts. The local church, an uncle's library, and the Great Salt Marshes had marked the confines of her daily existence. In her mind, she had traveled far beyond—to ancient Greece and Rome, to Elizabethan England, and to fabulous places that existed only in her imagination. But the upcoming trip to Cambridge was to be her first real entrée to the outside world. As a young woman, she would never be allowed to attend college. Still, the Harvard commencement would expose her to learned men and great ideas, abstract disquisitions and intense debates. For a short while she would be able to share—if only vicariously—her brother's role in that world.

In her enthusiasm for learning, Mercy was unlike most of her female contemporaries. Educated by a tutor along with James, she had consumed the classics of literature, mythology, and history—and begged for more. She had learned to write, and, with her brother's encouragement, she had begun to compose poetry. When he had left for college a few years earlier, she had been heartsick. He was her best friend and closest intellectual companion. Though he had written and visited home often, she missed his daily encouragement and constant companionship. Now, in 1743, she would see the happy results of their painful separation.

The Harvard commencement promised to offer great excitement to the entire Otis clan. Her father James, Sr., was as eager as Mercy to behold this day. Although locally successful as a lawyer, merchant, and farmer, he had never attended college. His son's graduation would affirm his own growing status and prominence in the community. But the event itself would be enjoyable and memorable. Indeed, in a colony whose ancestors were called "Puritans," public days of celebration were few and far between. As one of the largest and grandest holidays, commencement provided a rare occasion when the normally self-restrained colonists tolerated merrymaking. On commencement day itself, and intermittently for many days afterward, Cambridge was the site of a raucous revelry that still had about it a slightly forbidden air. People flocked to the town from all parts of New England. Tents were set up along the roads leading to and from the college. Before and after the solemn graduation exercises, graduates and guests indulged in all sorts of festivities—feasting, drinking, wrestling, cardplaying, and dancing. In a tightly controlled society, commencement also offered one of the few opportunities for young men and women to socialize freely. As a 1718 commencement poem put it, "Amorous Lads to shady Groves resort,/And under Venus with their Misses sport."

Mercy, too, had thoughts about "amorous lads." As unconventional as she was in some ways, she was in many respects a typical eighteenth-century adolescent girl. And like most women her age, she envisioned a future as a wife and a mother. For better or worse, she had few other choices. She knew that a woman's happiness hinged on her judicious selection of a companionable and financially secure mate. In every sense, her spouse's fate would become her own. It was thus not too early for Mercy to begin thinking about what kind of husband she wanted. And at James's graduation, she would encounter a variety of potential marital prospects.

As fate would have it, Mercy did indeed meet her future husband on one of those hot July days in Cambridge. Sandy-haired James Warren of Plymouth had become acquainted with James Otis when they both were undergraduates at Harvard. Sharing a lively wit and a mutual passion for politics, they had quickly become friends. It is likely that Otis introduced Warren to his favorite sister at one of the many postcommencement parties. Although it took eleven years for their acquaintance to blossom into marriage, Mercy remembered that James had appealed to her from the very start. He was, she said, a "powerful magnet, the center of my early wishes and the star which attracts my attention." She apparently never entertained any other serious suitors.

James's graduation, then, was nearly as significant in his sister's life as it was in his own. It also, however, reflected a powerful image of the dynamics that shaped Mercy's life. On that July day, Mercy was surrounded by the three most important influences in her life: her father, her brother, and her future husband. In a era in which women had no legal existence apart from their fathers or husbands, it is not surprising that three men should be pivotal to the young woman's development. But what made Mercy different from most other women of her generation was the way the men in her life treated her. Her father supported his daughter's wish for a highly unorthodox education, one more appropriate for a boy than a girl. Her brother cultivated his sister's native intellect, promoting her continuing self-education and eventually giving her access, through his own activities, to the world of politics. Her future husband James was perhaps the most unusual of all. He not only tolerated, but actually encouraged his wife's "unfeminine" interests in politics and writing. Ironically, Mercy Otis Warren came to be who she was because the men in her life allowed her to violate the established boundaries of womanhood. She could express her talents because they gave her the sanction to do so. Few other women of her time received such liberal dispensations.

* * *

A major part of Mercy's life was spent in the shadow of wars—wars that shaped the course of her life. During the first half of the century, the English and the French, aided by their Indian allies, struggled for control of the North American continent. Resolution of the struggle took many years. Although Queen Anne's War ended in a virtual stalemate in 1713, armed confrontation resumed in 1739 with the coming of King George's War. The peace, concluded in 1748, was brief. By 1754, the antagonists were at it again, this time in the climatic conflict known as the French and Indian War. During one of the few lulls in the fighting, on September 25, 1728, Mercy was born.

War also shaped some of her most outstanding childhood memories. An event occurring during King George's War proved to be particularly noteworthy. At 1:00 o'clock on the morning of July 3, 1745, bells in the West Barnstable meetinghouse pealed. As residents rushed out of their houses to hear the news, they learned that the alarm was not a warning of an imminent attack by their papist enemies, but word of a great victory. Over a month before, more than three thousand Massachusetts citizens had launched an assault on Fort Louisburg, the mightiest fortress in French Canada, indeed in all of North America. Fighting largely unaided by the mother country, often attacking from mere fishing boats, the colonists had vanquished the "Gibraltar of the New World." Providence, it seemed, had aided the godliest, most determined side. As it would later turn out, the colonists' mammoth effort had been for naught. Under the terms of the treaty ending the war, British negotiators returned the fort to the French. From that time on, some Americans began to wonder where Britain's true interests lay.

It would be many more years, however, before the Otises harbored such suspicions. Mercy's family was proud of their English identity and heritage. Their history recapitulated the prototypical tale of the colony's early settlement and development. On both sides, Mercy traced her ancestors back to some of the region's earliest settlers, the Puritans. As dissenters from the Church of England, the Puritans fled to the New World seeking an opportunity to associate with like-minded people and create a godly commonwealth on earth. Her mother's family found its roots in Edward Dotey, one of the signers of the Mayflower Compact and a founder of the Plymouth Colony. Over time, as the colony grew more crowded, Mercy's maternal grandfather decided to seek out better opportunities on the Connecticut frontier. He relocated the family to Wethersfield, where Mercy's mother was born. Her father's ancestors, on the other hand, had settled in Hingham, a town in the original Massachusetts Bay Colony. Arriving in 1631 as part of the Great Migration, the first Otises quickly accumulated substantial amounts of land and property. Seeking to expand his holdings, in 1683 Mercy's paternal grandfather moved to Barnstable, where he soon gained prominence as a leading merchant and politician. Her father James, born in 1702, capitalized on his father's substantial legacy. For the first generations of Puritans, the drive for economic self-improvement reinforced their religious zeal; worldly ambitions coexisted with divine aspirations.

By the time Mercy's parents were born, the tenor of life in Massachusetts already had changed considerably. In 1684, Britain revoked the Massachusetts Bay charter, a document that had given colonists great freedom to enforce their religious ideals through the mechanisms of the civil government. Under the new charter, Plymouth and Massachusetts Bay were joined into a single colony under royal jurisdiction. In the new government, the church possessed much less civil power and legal authority. Although Congregationalists, as the Puritans came to be known, still received preferential treatment, they now had to share their commonwealth with other religious groups, such as Quakers and Baptists. They no longer could dream of erecting a pure city on a hill, a model for the rest of the world to follow. By the turn of the century, although the colonists were not necessarily less spiritual than their ancestors, they no longer exhibited the single-ness of purpose or sense of religious unity that had character-ized the earlier settlement.

Time had also allowed the colony to prosper. No longer a struggling frontier community, Massachusetts was now one of the most populous of Britain's New World possessions. Al-though mostly small farmers, the colony's inhabitants pro-duced enough to feed themselves, often with enough left over to engage in local trade. In Boston, international trade and shipbuilding had made the city the largest urban center and most important port in the colonies. By the end of the seven-teenth century, Massachusetts merchants controlled 40 per-cent of the carrying capacity of all colonial-owned shipping. Although economic change may have heightened disparities between the rich and the poor in the capital, it raised the stan-dard of living for most citizens. By the mid-eighteenth cen-tury, the colonists enjoyed a level of comfort and material in-dulgence that would have stunned their forebears.

Despite profound changes altering the landscape of Massa-chusetts society, the seacoast town of Barnstable was something of a backwater, or to put it more positively, an island in the midst of the storm. Located about twenty-five miles southeast of Plymouth, most of Barnstable's eight hundred or so resi-dents supported themselves through farming, and, to a lesser extent, through small-scale shipping, whaling, or trading. Stable, homogeneous, and self-contained, the community, with the exception of a few elite families, tended to look inward rather than outward. As in many Massachusetts towns, a small group of families ruled the town government with a firm hand. Men from these families—the Bacons, Bourns, Gorhams, Lothrops, Thatchers, and Mercy's own family, the Otises— tended to be elected and reelected to positions in town and colonial government. Although attentive to their constituents' needs, representatives were thought to be independent of the people; their warrant came more from God than from the voters. Massachusetts was thus more democratic in form than in substance.

The people of Barnstable, moreover, tended to be conservative economically as well as politically. In 1740, the town's electors rejected a proposal for the creation of a land bank, an institution that would have generated a paper currency and eased the plight of debtors. Whatever its potential benefits, the Barnstable town meeting concluded that the bank represented a dangerous innovation that threatened to destabilize the economy and disrupt business as usual. They preferred to grapple with the known rather than take a risk on the unknown.

Unlike many other Massachusetts towns, Barnstable was still conservative in religious matters as well. It remained virtually untouched by the Great Awakening, the great religious revival that swept through the colonies in the 1740s. Featuring new, more emotional styles of preaching, sometimes delivered by nonresident, or itinerant ministers, the Awakening often proved to be a divisive force. Support for the Awakening often turned clergyman against clergyman, split congregations in two, or wrenched towns apart. In 1740, the most famous preacher of the revival, George Whitefield, ventured as close to Barnstable as Boston. But the Second Church in the East Parish of Barnstable remained a bulwark of orthodoxy. Congregants neither wanted nor needed outside preachers to stir them up to new heights of religious "enthusiasm"—a dirty word in those days. They preferred to practice a more traditional religion inherited from their Puritan forebears, a religion of duty, discipline, and rationality. The Barnstable of Mercy's youth, then, was a safe, predictable place where the outside world did not much intrude.

Mercy's parents were stalwart citizens of that world. In 1724, James Otis had brought Mary Allyne of Wethersfield, Connecticut, home to be his bride. They were each only twenty-two years old. In the small world of Barnstable, Mercy's family stood near the top rung of society. Her grandfather and father were prominent figures in business and local politics. Fortunately for Mercy, her father, though the youngest son, had inherited from his father substantial lands and the family homestead. Overlooking Barnstable's Great Salt Marshes, near Cape Cod Bay, the house was described at the time as a "high double house with a gambrel roof and three dormer windows." Outside, huge buttonwood trees shaded the yard and provided firewood for the family—fifty cords would keep the fireplaces roaring through the winter. Possibly to accommodate a growing family, possibly to announce his increasing social status, James added two wings to the building. Inside, mahogany chests, elaborate mirrors, and one of the first clocks in the county graced the house. Reflecting the colonists' growing appetite for luxury goods, the Otises purchased pewter plates, engraved silver bowls, and damask tablecloths. The children slept on feather beds and ate with silverware. Although Mercy grew up in comfort, she did not live in splendor. The Otises were large fish in a small pond.

Like many other New Englanders, Mary and James were eager to have many children. The Otises, however, were unluckier than most. At a time when the infant mortality rate was about 25 percent, six of the family's thirteen children did not live to adulthood. In this situation, religion provided a needed measure of consolation and comfort. If, as Puritans believed, death was God's will, then individuals must accept the pain, resign themselves to the inevitable, and meditate on the event as a way of increasing their own godliness. Still, each of the deaths engendered a profound sense of loss and caused the Otises to grieve afresh. A sensitive child, Mercy no doubt found the episodes traumatic.

Notwithstanding the frequency of the deaths of her infant siblings, Mercy grew up in a fairly typical Puritan home. Her parents regarded their family as a "little commonwealth," a microcosm of the larger society and an agent for inculcating religious values. Together, Mercy's parents exercised unquestioned authority over their children. In accordance with good Calvinistic doctrine, they attempted to vanquish sin, extirpate any signs of their children's willfulness, and teach them the way to salvation. Sparing the rod, they feared, might spoil the child. Although Mercy's parents most assuredly loved her, they expressed that love in the form of discipline rather than affection. This method left some scars. Much later, Mercy explicitly repudiated the "Irksome Methods of Severity" that had characterized her upbringing. She did not want to inflict the excesses of the "evangelical mode" of childrearing, as historian Philip Greven has called it, on her own children.

But the Otis family exhibited domestic arrangements typical for the time. Although hierarchical and patriarchal in structure, the Puritan family also assigned a dignified place to women. As wife and mother, the woman was regarded as the husband's essential friend, companion, and helpmeet. While she must defer to her husband, she had a particular realm of authority of her own—the household.

In the eighteenth century, running a successful household depended enormously on the efficiency of the women in the house. In keeping with the Otises' relatively high social status, several servants, including a black slave, assisted Mary Allyne Otis in performing the domestic chores and taking care of the children. Yet the ultimate responsibility for the household fell largely on the mistress herself: she had to do many jobs personally or supervise the servants closely. These chores were burdensome, demanding, and physically exhausting. Each day the women servants and female family members had to milk the cows, build the fires, prepare and cook the meals. Clothes, sometimes made from thread and fabric made by the women themselves, had to be sewn and washed. On larger farms, women might produce other goods—candles, cheese, or butter—that could be used by the family or traded for other useful items.

Strong taboos prevented the men, even the boys, from helping the women do their work. So it was up to Mrs. Otis, her four daughters, and the female servants to keep the Otis house functioning. As the third child and eldest daughter, Mercy bore an especially heavy burden. During Mary's many pregnancies and postpartum recovery periods, Mercy increasingly acted as her mother's "deputy" and assumed many of Mary's duties around the house. In the process, she learned the practical skills that would one day enable her to become the efficient mistress of her own household. Mercy also learned about the rigors of motherhood. The birth of ten younger siblings initiated Mercy into the female-centered rituals surrounding childbirth and prepared her for the day when she too would have children.

Mercy's mother also passed on to her daughter more sophisticated skills. For good Puritan men and women, reading the Bible was an essential part of religious education and a staple of devotional practice. The rate of female literacy in New England was high—perhaps as high as 70 percent in the early eighteenth century. It is likely, then, that Mary taught her daughters how to read, as well as instructed them in the feminine arts. Embroidery, for example, was a skill thought to be both useful and aesthetically pleasing. Mary no doubt spent many hours demonstrating the stitches and supervising her daughter's efforts. Mercy, it seems, enjoyed and even excelled at this task. Contemporaries remarked on the beauty of an elaborately embroidered satin dress that she wore the day after her wedding. And even today the Plymouth Pilgrim's Hall Museum displays Mercy's intricately stitched, brightly colored cardtable cover, a work that reveals both her fine sense of detail as well as her mastery of a difficult craft.

Despite Mary's significance in Mercy's life, the mother never seemed to figure largely in her daughter's affections, at least as Mercy recorded them on paper as an adult. Mercy never referred to her mother in her existing letters, nor did she write a poem commemorating her death in 1767, as she did for several other family members. All the Otis children seem to have regarded their mother as a remote and moody figure. The fact that Mrs. Otis bore thirteen children and buried six of them might reasonably account for her melancholy. Whatever the cause, Mercy's relationship with her mother never evinced the warmth she felt toward her father, with whom she was demonstrably close.

Colonel James Otis, as he was called, exercised his authority over his family with a firm hand. Even Mercy spoke of her father's control in terms of a "patriarchship." At times, his domineering character seems to have caused tensions between him and his sons. But James seems to have had a special fondness for his eldest daughter, who reciprocated his sentiments and took care of him in his later years. She often referred to him as her "venerated father."

Colonel James was a man of great native intelligence, substantial charm, and immense energy. Although he had not attended college, he was a quick learner and a man of vision. He wanted to be more than a simple farmer. Soon after taking up residence on the family lands, he began to direct his prodigious energies toward gilding the family dynasty. Aggressively setting out to improve his status and wealth, he expanded the family storehouse, sought out new trading partners, and invested in new business endeavors, such as whaling. In 1730, he branched off in an entirely new direction, by establishing himself in the practice of law.

At this time, lawyers required no special schooling or licensing; any literate man could practice law. As he gained experience, Colonel James proved to have a special knack for litigation. Although he handled some criminal cases, he found himself increasingly involved in civil matters—the recovery of debts, the mediation of property disputes, and the arbitration of wills. Always seeking to expand his clientele, Otis rode the circuit to neighboring towns and villages. In little more than a decade, he came to represent nearly half the litigants bringing suit at the Barnstable County Court. These endeavors brought him success. Not only did he earn substantial fees (as much as £1,200 per year), he also gained the confidence and acquaintance of many people, becoming the center of an influential network that extended throughout Barnstable County. These contacts enabled him to invest in lucrative trading ventures and, eventually, to make his way into politics.

Despite his frequent absences from the household, Colonel James apparently took a strong interest in his eldest daughter. At some point, perhaps when she was nine or ten, he granted permission for Mercy to be educated by a private tutor along with her older brothers. We can only speculate on the precise course of events that led to this rather unorthodox decision. Like other girls in New England, Mercy had learned to read at an early age. But the education of many women stopped there. Writing was regarded as a vocational skill needed only by males; many females never learned to write.

Mercy, however, yearned to learn more than just the basics. A girl of great curiosity and enthusiasm, she sensed there was a wider world awaiting her. She watched enviously as her two older brothers, James and Joseph, went off to school—not to Barnstable's public grammar school, but for tutoring with their uncle, a Yale-trained minister. The Reverend Jonathan Russell provided the boys with a rigorous classical education that would prepare them for college. Mercy, too, had visited her Uncle Russell's house many times. When she entered his study, lined with hundreds of books containing the accumulated wisdom of theology, philosophy, history, and natural science, her skin would prickle in anticipation. She longed to touch the leather volumes, hold them in her hands, devour their contents. But girls were not supposed to want such things.

Fortunately, her brother James knew of Mercy's interests. Acknowledging her precocity, he took an active hand in encouraging her intellectual development. Together they explored the labyrinthine excesses of Greek mythology, exulted in the heroic achievements of the Roman republic, and plumbed the delicate intricacies of Shakespeare's sonnets. He didn't seem to mind that Mercy was a girl; he treated her as an intellectual equal. At some point, the siblings must have wondered why Mercy, who was so quick and clever, did not also attend school at their Uncle Russell's house. Soon thereafter, Mercy began to go to school with her brothers.

Under Russell's tutelage, Mercy obtained a rigorous, classical education. Because she would not be going to college, she was not instructed in Greek or Latin. But in most other ways, she was treated as one of the boys. She studied Greek and Roman literature in translation, learned ancient and modern history, and explored the works of English authors such as Shakespeare, Pope, Dryden, and Milton. She also learned to write. Not only did she absorb the basic elements of composition, she perfected a subtle and refined prose style capable of conveying complex notions and learned ideas.

Mercy's education provided her with more than just intellectual knowledge; it shaped her image of herself. In the Reverend Russell's study, she demonstrated that she was as quick and competent as her brothers. She could write as well as they could, hold her own in discussion, and master the same subjects. She gained the boys' respect as they gained hers. In the process, she began to have some of the same aspirations as they did. She came to love politics and the study of history. Raleigh's *History of the World* was said to be one of her favorite works. She began to have a literary bent—or at least to realize that she could express herself through literary means. Over time, she would turn more deliberately to these avenues of expression. For now, she gloried in the realization that in the realm of ideas, gender was no barrier to equality. To their credit, the men of her family did not disabuse her of that notion.

Mercy's bond with her brother James deepened over the years. Three and one-half years her senior, Jemmy, as he was called, was her closest friend, her trusted companion, and constant adviser. Although she had younger sisters, it was to Jemmy that Mercy turned in times of trouble or distress. When he left for college, he continued to supervise her reading and offer his support for her endeavors. She loved him dearly.

In subsequent years, Jemmy would become one of the first, most articulate, but also one of the most erratic leaders of the revolutionary movement. After graduating from Harvard in 1743, he returned home to Barnstable. Following a traditional path, he studied privately for two years in order to obtain his Master's Degree. A brilliant classicist, he published a book on Latin prosody and completed a manuscript on Greek prosody. He then went off to Boston to read law with one of the most prominent attorneys of the day, Jeremiah Gridley. He immersed himself in the English common law tradition and read the great legal theorists: Pufendorf, Gortius, Vatell, and Justinian, among others. With his razor-sharp mind and stubborn intensity, Jemmy mastered his studies quickly. In 1748 he moved to Plymouth, where he established his own legal practice. Though successful in winning cases, he was not as successful in attracting clients. On at least two separate occasions, father and son tangled with each other in court. Representing opposite sides, in both instances the fancily educated son triumphed over the self-educated father. Nonetheless, Colonel James had more work than he could handle, while the son could barely make a living. For the younger Otis, the pursuit of abstract legalisms was far more interesting than the pursuit of potential clients, a necessary step in building a small-town legal practice.

Jemmy also seems to have needed a broader canvas on which to display his talents. In 1750, the young attorney returned to Boston to seek his fortune. He acted as his father's agent—shopping for goods, arranging for shipments, representing him in certain legal matters. He also built on his connections from Harvard to forge a flourishing legal practice. Soon he represented various prominent merchants from such eminent families as the Hancocks, the Vassals, and the Halls. Ingratiating himself with royal officials, he also acquired a variety of minor, and not so minor, political appointments. By the 1760s, he began to emerge as a leading spokesman of the opposition party and one of the first proponents of American rights in the face of British oppression.

As Jemmy achieved success, and then notoriety, in the realm of politics, he brought Mercy along with him on his intellectual journey. Their frequent correspondence allowed her to keep abreast of the rapidly changing political scene and her brother's evolving views. Their mutual affection never waned. "This you may depend on," he told her in 1766. "No man ever loved a sister better, and among all my conflicts I never forget that I am endeavoring to serve you and yours." By the late 1760s, an encroaching insanity made Jemmy increasingly unpredictable and irresponsible. Mercy worried about him constantly: he was, she told him in 1771, "the continual subject both of my sleeping and waking thoughts." Although she acknowledged his faults, Mercy regarded her eldest brother as a flawed genius, one "whose superior abilities are such that with a calm and steady mind, he is capable of promoting the greatest good to his fellow creatures—and in consequence thereof to secure to himself eternal felicity." She ignored or tried to explain away his eccentricities. She assumed his political passions as her own and followed his logic down its tortuous path. When he was no longer able to wage the fight against British tyranny, she picked up the gauntlet. Their bond transcended that of brother and sister; it became a merger of two exceptional intellects and wills.

Yet Jemmy's relationship with Mercy had transformed him as well as her. His sister's brilliance led him to an unfashionable belief in the equality of the sexes. From personal experience, he knew that with the proper encouragement and opportunity women could attain intellectual parity with men. In the 1760s, he oversaw the education of a young girl who would one day write the first American novel, *Charlotte Temple*.

As a close friend of the family, he had recognized the incipi-
ent genius of the young Susanna Haswell Rowson and promoted it. Jemmy also went public with his views on women's
equality. In his 1764 pamphlet, *The Rights of the British Colonies Asserted and Proved*, he asked, "Are not women born as
free as men? Would it not be infamous to assert that the ladies are all slaves by nature? . . . If upon the abdication [of
James II] all were reduced to a state of nature, had not apple
women and orange girls as good a right to give their respectable suffrages for a new King as . . . the politician?" Unfortunately, his dedication to Mercy also may have had other, less
fortunate consequences. It seems no accident that Jemmy did
not marry until six months after his sister had done so. Even
then, although he wed a wealthy, beautiful woman named
Ruth Cunningham, with whom he had three children, his
relationship with his wife never appeared as fulfilling as his
connection with his sister.

As important as Jemmy was to Mercy's life, she would not
have had a career as a writer without the support and encouragement of her husband, James Warren. Warren hailed from
a family at least as prominent in Plymouth as Mercy's family
was in Barnstable. He, too, traced his ancestors back to the
Mayflower. His family, too, engaged in a profitable mixture of
agriculture and trading. Born in 1726, Warren, as the eldest
son, expected to inherit the largest portion of his father's estate. After his graduation from Harvard in 1745, he appren-
ticed himself to his father in anticipation of that day.

From the first day that Mercy laid eyes on James Warren at
her brother's graduation until her wedding day, more than a
decade passed. Although we do not know the details of their
courtship, we can reasonably speculate on the course of events.
It seems likely that Jemmy reintroduced his friend to his sister
in 1748 or 1749, while he was living in Plymouth, Warren's
hometown. The courtship was likely to have occurred under
the watchful eyes of Mercy's family. James probably visited her
in Barnstable. To get to know one another, they may have

strolled around the Great Salt Marshes, attended barnraisings, or accompanied one another to church services. Because Warren lived in a different town, he even may have spent the night at the Otis household occasionally. Under these circumstances, some New England families allowed a courting couple to sleep in the same bed—fully clothed with a "bundling board" separating them. (Such precautions seem to have had limited success in preventing intimate contact between the bundled bedmates. The rate of prenuptial pregnancies skyrocketed around this time.) The Otis home, however, was sufficiently large so as to preclude the necessity for such an arrangement.

Eventually, they decided to marry. Once Mercy and James made their decision, they issued the banns, a public announcement of their intentions. Following an ancient custom, they posted the banns three times on the door to Mercy's parish, at the West Barnstable Meetinghouse. Yet the wedding itself would not be a religious affair. Unlike Anglicans and Roman Catholics, Puritans believed that marriage was a civil contract rather than a religious sacrament. Consequently, a magistrate rather than a minister would preside over the actual ceremony.

Mercy Otis wed James Warren on November 14, 1754. November was the favorite month for Puritan weddings; by that time of the year the community's inhabitants had finished the work of the busy harvest season but had not yet begun the preparations for the spring planting. Both parties were somewhat older than the norm: she was 26, at a time when women in Massachusetts usually married at 23, and he was 28, at a time when men usually married at 26. Yet like many other Massachusetts sons, Warren had wanted to postpone marriage until he had reached his late twenties, when, he figured, he would have the means to establish a family of his own. As it turned out, however, James did not receive his full inheritance for several more years, until after his father had passed away.

On the day of the wedding, members of the two families and a few close friends gathered at the Otis family house. In a brief service, the couple exchanged vows. A restrained celebration followed, at which guests were treated to a hearty wedding dinner, bridal cakes, and cups of sack posset (a wine punch that was used to toast the bridal couple). In keeping with Puritan decorum, there was no excessive drinking and no dancing at the reception. Soon after dinner, the assembled guests sang a psalm and the newlyweds excused themselves. The ancient custom of charivari encouraged friends to tease and taunt the newlyweds, even as they secreted themselves in the bridal chamber. Shortly after the wedding day, Mercy and James moved into the Warren family home at Eel River near Plymouth.

The two had wed at a time when older, more functionalistic notions of marriage were giving way to more romantic, companionate conceptions. Mercy and James's relationship reflected the influence of both the older and newer ideas about marriage. While they experienced a deep affection for and strong attraction to one another, they also shared a common social, economic, and religious background and held similar values. Both were highly principled, even to the point of rigidity and self-righteousness. Both had cut their teeth on politics and retained a life-long fascination with the affairs of state. Both even had a common ancestor, a certain great-great-grandfather named Edward Dotey.

As the descendants of Puritans, both Warrens shared a firm belief in God. Unlike their ancestors, however, their belief tended to be more rationalistic, restrained, and stoic rather than fervent and all-consuming. While spirituality shaped the contours of their mental outlook, their daily life tended to be centered on more earthly concerns. As children of the Enlightenment, they also shared a love of nature. Galileo and Newton had shown that nature operated according to certain predictable laws; the universe was not a random occurrence. The Warrens saw no necessary contradiction between faith and reason, as one of Mercy's poems made clear:

> Not even Newton's godlike mind,
> Nor all the sages of mankind,

Could e'er assign another cause,
Though much they talk of nature's laws. . . .

All perfect wisdom still directs
Their revolutions;—knows the hour
When rapid times resist less pow'r,
In mighty ruin will involve,
And God—this grand machine dissolve.

Science, as the Warrens saw it, might explain the natural order, but God still directed it. In addition, they enjoyed the
aesthetic pleasures provided by nature. James frequently expressed his contentment with the agrarian life. Like George
Washington, Thomas Jefferson, and many other patriots of
the founding era, he was a gentleman farmer who liked nothing better than to contemplate new systems of crop rotation,
experiment with exotic seedlings, or read "Tull's fine
Phylosophical System of Vegetation." For Mercy, the appeal of
nature was "beauteous and sublime" rather than scientific, providing her with a reservoir of peace or a reminder of the awe-
someness of divine power.

Whatever the constraints of a hierarchical and patriarchal
society, Mercy and James enjoyed a partnership grounded in
mutuality and reciprocity. Mercy often referred to James as
the "first friend of my heart." Throughout a series of personal
crises and disappointments in the 1780s and 1790s, she unerr-
ingly supported him and took his side in public disputes. "Your
father," Mercy wrote her eldest son in 1797, "is the philoso-
pher and the Christian:—he is the best husband, the best father—the best friend." She frequently expressed her affection
for and dependence on him. "All my Earthly Happiness," she
wrote to him in 1772, "depend[s] on the continuance of [your]
Life."

James felt the same way about his beloved wife. "How can I
love and esteem you enough," he proclaimed during the Revolution, "and yet no Husband ever loved and respected a Wife

more?" At a time when it was most unusual for women to think about politics or have literary aspirations, he actively supported her efforts and cherished her unique talents and abilities. As Mercy was preparing her first book for publication, he wrote, "I suppose you are busily Engaged in the Business of an Author of great Abilities, discernment & Judgment, yet diffident & therefore hunting for Criticism & advise & correcting the draft with a trembling heart. If you had half the good opinion of yourself that I have of you[,] you certainly would not feel half the anxiety that You do now." Secure in his own talents, he freely acknowledged her superiority to him in certain arenas. Later in her life, Mercy would often experience debilitating depressions and physical ailments. Through it all, James would patiently try to cajole her into good spirits and facilitate the expression of her genius. "[A] brilliant and Busy Imagination often if not always Accompanys great qualities," he observed in 1779. "It Commands Admiration but is often Mischievous and when yours is not directed to the bright side of things, I often wish it as Sluggish as my own, but I long to Banter and Laugh you out of your whimsical Gloom." As exceptional as Mercy was, only an exceptional husband could have enabled her to express her talents.

The marriage of Mercy Otis and James Warren was notable for its intimacy, passion, and mutual respect. In their fifty-four year union, they produced five children and weathered numerous personal and professional crises. Although their love for one another never seemed to waver, even an idyllic relationship took work. Writing to her newly married daughter-in-law, Mercy observed, "Many of our thoughtless sex as soon as the connubial knot is tied, neglect the continual attention (which is necessary without discovering the exertion) to keep the *sacred flame* of love alive." Both Warrens seemed committed to doing the hard work necessary to sustain the "sacred flame of love."

* * *

Mercy Otis Warren's early years contain only a few hints of the unconventional path her life would later take. Certain men— most especially, her father, her brother, and her husband— recognized from early on that she was a woman of exceptional talents and ability. Through them, she received an unusually good education, access to the world of politics, and the encouragement to write. In the 1750s and 1760s, Mercy Otis Warren envisioned her life much as other women at the time did. What she wanted most of all was to be a good wife, an efficient housemistress, and a loving mother. Despite a flair with the pen, her writing might well have remained a private hobby or a curious feminine affectation. In the mid-1760s, however, an extraordinary series of political events began to unfold. These events would eventually propel her—as an Otis, a Warren, and a woman—into the public realm.

CHAPTER TWO

Politics as a Family Affair

In Mercy Otis Warren's time, politics was a man's affair. Both men and women believed that it was right and proper for men to govern. Women were officially shut out from the polling place, from the legislative chamber, even from public discussions of political issues. Women who interested themselves in such matters ran the risk of being labelled "manly" and would, it was thought, assume masculine characteristics. Only at their own peril did women cross the invisible boundary that demarcated appropriate behavior for their sex.

For Mercy, however, politics was the favorite family sport. She had cut her teeth hearing about her father's involvement in town, county, and colonywide politics. Her brother Jemmy was a political animal as well. As an adult, he roared onto the Massachusetts political scene and became one of the leaders of the popular, or opposition party. Her husband eventually entered the political fray as well. Whether she wanted to be or not, Mercy was never far removed from the tempestuous political issues of the day.

These experiences provided Mercy with a political education. The 1760s would prove to be an especially turbulent time in Massachusetts politics. Over the course of the decade, Mercy watched as her family's political affairs became entangled first with royal officials in Massachusetts, then with England itself. Familial politics became imperial politics. Observing the political process at close quarters, she followed her friends and relatives as they developed a logic of resistance. Through her father and brother, she imbibed a personal antagonism toward one of the most important representatives of royal authority in the colony, Thomas Hutchinson. Through Jemmy and her husband, she witnessed firsthand the developing alienation between the colonies and Great Britain. Through John Adams, Samuel Adams, and others, she saw colonial leaders plot the means and strategies of protest, experienced with them the victory of success, felt with them the frustration of failure. Like them, she grew increasingly suspicious of Britain's motives and methods. In the 1760s, Mercy became a revolutionary by association.

* * *

Though luckier than many, the Warrens' early wedded years proceeded much like that of other young people in Massachusetts at the time. After their wedding, Mercy and James moved in with James's father at the family's Eel River farm near Plymouth. Like many other New England sons, James was dependent on his father for his status and means of livelihood. In many ways, the timing of his inheritance structured James's life: it probably delayed his marriage to Mercy by a few years, and it may have delayed the couple's decision to have children. After James's father died in 1757, a series of events occurred: James inherited the Eel River property, which Mercy renamed "Clifford"; the family purchased an additional house in the nearby town of Plymouth; and Mercy became pregnant with their first child. Over the years, Mercy would bear five sons, henceforth in rapid succession: James, on Oct 18, 1757; Winslow, on March 24, 1759; Charles, on April 14, 1762; Henry, on March 21, 1764; and George, on September 20, 1766.

The late 1750s and 1760s thus represented a time in which family concerns were paramount in Mercy's life. Like other women of her day, she no doubt approached childbirth with a mixture of excitement and apprehension. In eighteenth-century New England, nearly one in four babies died at birth or soon thereafter; one in every two hundred women did not survive the experience. Even after a successful delivery, the mother was still in danger. Many died of puerperal fever, a bacterial infection of the uterine cavity, which could develop shortly after birthing. Yet for Mercy, the experience of childbirth went smoothly. She came through the births in fine health, and none of her children died in infancy or childhood.

For Mercy, as for other women, the birth of a child represented an important rite of passage—a female-centered ritual that marked a woman's entry into full adulthood. During the early stages of labor, according to historian Laurel Thatcher Ulrich, the atmosphere among the attending women resembled a party. Male family members were sent away, as female friends and relatives gathered at the expectant mother's house to provide support, advice, and encouragement. They refreshed themselves with special drinks and foods, preparing "groaning beer" and "groaning cakes" for the occasion. They urged the mother-to-be to eat lightly and walk around during the early stages of labor.

At this time, childbirth was neither a secretive nor a highly clinical event. As farm dwellers, the colonists had from childhood observed animals in the process of procreation. Because their houses were so small (on average 3 or 4 rooms), parents had little privacy from their children. Older girls, such as Mercy, often witnessed their mothers giving birth to younger siblings. In any case, birth was regarded as a natural process. When it became clear that a birth was imminent, or if the laboring woman was in extreme distress, a midwife would be summoned. Although they lacked the formal schooling of physicians, midwives were highly skilled and quite competent in bringing mother and child through a healthy delivery. During the birthing process, the midwife might provide the mother with medicinal herbs to ease the pain, massage her stomach or perineum, turn the baby's head and shoulders, or cut the umbilical cord at the appropriate time.

The weeks after giving birth were at once joyous and exhausting. Although Mercy had domestic servants who kept the household running while she was indisposed, she probably did not spend much time "lying in," as it was called. Within weeks, or even days, after delivery she resumed her duties as mistress of the household. As her brood grew, her mothering responsibilities multiplied. But eighteenth-century women used a natural mechanism to help space their children. Mothers often breastfed their children until they were at least one, and often two, years old. Prolonged lactation functioned as a natural fertility inhibitor. In an era lacking in artificial contraception, breastfeeding helped limit family size. Mercy's own children were born at regular intervals ranging from seventeen to thirty-seven months, with a mean of nearly two years, suggesting that breastfeeding played a role in determining her childbearing pattern as well.

Mercy took her role as mother quite seriously. She read widely in an effort to find the most thoughtful approach to childrearing. "I am yet looking," she told Abigail Adams, "for every foreign aid to enable me to discharge a duty of the highest consequence to society." Rather than focus on children's sinfulness and capacity for evil, Mercy concentrated on their goodness and potential for reason and virtue. Children, she told Abigail in 1774, are "tender plants" that one must "cultivate" in order "to become useful in their departments,—an ornament to society, and happy themselves *forever.*" Affectionate persuasion rather than coercive discipline characterized her approach.

Mercy's attitude toward her children reflected an explicit rejection of her parents' harsh Calvinistic methods toward children. Over time, she had absorbed the more temperate, rational approach conveyed by a variety of Enlightenment tracts. In part, Mercy consulted popular manuals, such as a work by Mrs. Seymour, which gave practical advice about clothing, chores, and discipline. But she also probably read John Locke's treatises on education and his *Essay on Human Understanding*, which articulated the broader theoretical assumptions that revolutionized the popular understanding of human intellectual growth and moral development. Locke maintained that the human mind at birth was blank and malleable, a tabula rasa. Children possessed enormous potential for both good and evil. As such, it was up to parents to inculcate sound values in their children and shape their ideas. Childrearing methods, he suggested, should be directed not toward eradicating children's inherent sinfulness or willfulness, but toward molding their minds and character in an enlightened fashion.

Enlightenment sources also provided Mercy with a new understanding of the dignity of motherhood and of women's importance to the family and society. Scottish philosophers such as Thomas Reid and James Fordyce discussed the role of women in maintaining the "little society" of the family and the social implications of what they called "politeness," the mechanism that made social intercourse possible. Adam Smith's *Theory of Moral Sentiments* and David Hume's various essays presented a new sociological understanding of the family, which acknowledged that a citizen's political socialization took place at a very early age, well before a person reached voting age. Other works highlighted the woman's role in the civilizing process. Baron de Montesquieu's *Spirit of Laws* and Lord Kames's *Six Sketches on the History of Man* offered a complex theory of historical development in which all societies progressed through four stages of evolution: from the earliest hunter phase, societies eventually passed into a pastoral era, which led to an agricultural stage, which in turn yielded to a commercial era. In each stage, social evolution both benefitted women, by increasing their status, and depended on them. Women softened men's animalistic passions and refined their brutish manners. In the fourth phase, the mercantile stage, women came into their own. No longer were they regarded merely as sex objects, but, according to Kames, as men's "faithful friends and agreeable companions." At this level, society accorded women a modicum of equality with men, not political equality by any means, but a kind of social equality that they had never before possessed.

This literature, read in conjunction with her own experience, convinced Mercy to become an eloquent advocate of women's education. Like many other thinkers of the late eighteenth century, Mercy assumed that men and women possessed equal capacity for intellectual development. Any evidence to the contrary resulted from a lack of sufficient educational opportunity. As she herself could testify, "The deficiency lies not so much in the inferior contexture of female intellects as in the different education bestowed on the sexes; for when the cultivation of the mind, in the early part of life is neglected in either, we see ignorance, stupidity, and ferocity of manners, equally conspicuous in both." Women, she said, echoing Kames, should be raised to the level of "friends" and "rational companions to men of understanding and taste."

But Mercy, like Locke, Kames, and others, understood that the woman's role did not end in the home. As wives and mothers, their influence was far-reaching. Because women were responsible for educating children in their earliest years, they had the most profound impact on them. "The early traits are seldom eradicated from the breasts of those who must tread the stage and regulate both the political and religious affairs of human life," she observed in a letter to her niece, Sally Sever. Male children, she noted, would grow up to be the future soldiers and statesmen of the republic. Thus a mother's influence and deportment "may have consequences that we cannot calculate. Not only our own families but society have a just claim on that sex whose peculiar province it is to plant the first rudiments of education in the infant mind, and to culti-

vate those principles of reason and rectitude [in children]."
For a variety of reasons, then, Mercy insisted, society must
choose to educate its women. Historian Linda Kerber has labelled this cluster of ideas "Republican Motherhood." As she
explains it, women's activities during the Revolution compelled
many people, both male and female, to come to a new realization about the role and status of women in society. As wives
and mothers, women were seen to make an important, though
indirect, contribution to the polity. Motherhood essentially
assumed a political, or protopolitical, function. Mercy Otis
Warren's writings suggest that the roots of the concept go
deeper. Republican Motherhood may have originated well before the Revolution—in both the abstract discourse of male
Enlightenment intellectuals and in the everyday experiences
of American wives and mothers. Although the Revolution probably made more people receptive, at least some women, including Mercy Warren, had arrived at the notion before the
first shot was fired.

Despite her scholarly disposition, Mercy did not lack maternal solicitude. Throughout her children's lives, she constantly instructed, cajoled, encouraged, and corrected them.
As her sons grew up and moved away from home, she corresponded with them frequently. Expressing the fears of generations of mothers everywhere, she once commented to her
eldest child, "When I consider how easily the generality of youth
are misled, either by novel opinions or unprincipled companions, and how easily they often glide into the path of folly, and
how imperceptibly they are led into the mazes of error; I
tremble for my children." Yet as they matured, she treated her
sons as her friends as well as children. In a letter to her sec-
ond-eldest, Winslow, in December 1779, she noted, "I write
with the warm emotions of maternal tenderness, strengthened
by the reciprocal tie of friendship and confidence (a light in
which at a certain stage I wish to view my sons)." She was never
happier than in the presence of her whole family—an occur-

rence that became increasingly rare over the years. She tolerated her sons' absences, knowing that only in the larger world could they fulfill themselves and bring to fruition the "seeds" she had planted. "I hope I shall live to see my dispersed family again collected under the parental roof," she wrote to George in 1784. "We miss you exceedingly . . . —but we acquiesce in the present dispersion hoping our promising sons will reap advantages in proportion to the self denial we feel by absence." Mercy strove, not always successfully, to balance her own desire for family togetherness with her sons' need for independence.

One strong thread linked Mercy's created family with the family of her birth, a preoccupation with politics and the affairs of state. In both the Otis and the Warren households, family members were important players in the political events of the day. They constantly discussed political ideas and affairs, including the machinations of the Massachusetts assembly, strategies of resistance to British authority, or the colonists' right to revolution. Whether or not she was personally involved, Mercy could not help but be informed of the changing nature of the political scene. This environment provided her with a superb political education.

As a child, Mercy watched as her father launched his studied entry into political life. Starting out as a country lawyer, he soon moved into local positions of importance, becoming hogreeve (a local administrator) in 1739 and a town selectman in 1744. In 1745, voters chose him as their delegate to the Massachusetts House of Representatives, a position he would hold for eleven straight years and intermittently thereafter. During the late 1740s, Colonel Otis strengthened his power—and not incidentally, his purse—by becoming an ally of Governor William Shirley. He suffered a setback in 1756, when he failed to win a seat on the Governor's Council. But in 1760, his constituents reelected him to the lower House, in which he was promptly chosen to be Speaker. Clearly, Mercy's father was a shrewd political manipulator who proved himself a survivor in the competitive, factionalized world of Massachusetts politics.

His son Jemmy also seemed to be an astute player in the minefield that was Massachusetts politics. Soon after moving to Boston, he began to move in elite circles. Through his connections, he secured various patronage positions. In 1756 he gained an appointment as a justice of the peace for Suffolk County. Soon thereafter, he became a deputy advocate-general of the Vice-Admiralty Court, a post that gave him significant influence in the legal affairs of the colony as well as a substantial annual stipend of £200. Continuing to cultivate his private law practice, Jemmy became known as a brilliant and vocal defender of the Boston merchant community.

But at the very same time that the Otises were consolidating their political power, another man was penetrating the political thickets. This man would hinder the Otises' quest for power, impugn their reputations, and stymie their hold over the legislature. He came to be the mortal enemy of James Otis Junior and Senior, and later, of Mercy herself. Eventually, this foe of the Otises', though a native of Massachusetts, would come to personify the threat of British tyranny in the colony. In her *History of the American Revolution*, Mercy would characterize this man in the most vitriolic terms:

> Few ages have produced a more fit instrument for the purposes of a corrupt court. He was dark, intriguing, insinuating, haughty, and ambitious, while the extreme of avarice marked every feature of his character. His abilities were little elevated above the line of mediocrity; yet by dint of industry, exact temperance, and indefatigable labor, he became master of the accomplishments necessary to acquire popular fame. . . . He had . . . diligently studied the intricacies of *Machiavelian* policy, and never failed to recommend the Italian master as a model to his adherents.

This man was Thomas Hutchinson.

Like the elder Otis, Hutchinson had come into prominence through Governor Shirley's patronage. After having served in various local offices and on the Governor's Council, in 1756 Hutchinson became Shirley's chief agent for military affairs, the liaison responsible for the colony's conduct in the French and Indian War. Having acquitted himself with distinction in this capacity, he was rewarded with the colony's lieutenant governorship. Ambitious, restrained, stern, and self-righteous, Hutchinson always had more supporters in England than in his native country.

Early in Hutchinson's career, the Otises felt no particular enmity toward the man. Colonel James had, on occasion, made common cause with him for political purposes. Jemmy courted him at times for favors. Yet a closely related series of events changed all that. In 1757, Colonel James, in anticipation of gaining a position on the more prestigious Governor's Council, resigned his seat in the House of Representatives. His desired appointment depended on the approval of the lower house, in which, of course, he had been a prominent leader. To his shock and disappointment, however, when the votes were counted, he fell short; his former colleagues had denied him the post. As he sought to determine the reasons for his failure, he discovered that Hutchinson had mounted a private whispering campaign against him. From that time on, the Otises regarded Hutchinson with increasing suspicion.

Subsequent events poisoned their relations for good. In 1760, the position of chief justice of the Massachusetts Superior Court was open. Several years earlier, Governor Shirley had promised Colonel James the next available position on the court. The new governor, Francis Bernard, did not, however, feel bound by his predecessor's promises. Instead, he invited Thomas Hutchinson to sit on the court.

Now the Otis family felt betrayed and humiliated. Not only had Colonel James not received the position, but their chief foil—who was not even a lawyer—had won out. In addition, the Otises viewed Hutchinson's appointment as the harbinger of a dangerous trend. Hutchinson already held several other official positions: he was a judge on the Suffolk probate court; a member of the Governor's Council; and the colony's lieutenant governor. At this time, although multiple office-holding was not illegal, the Otises argued that the situation created an insidious concentration of power in the hands of one person. To make matters worse (in their eyes), Hutchinson was related by marriage to another powerful family, the Olivers, who occupied many key governmental positions in the colony. The Otises' arch rival thus possessed an invisible network of influence that held the entire Massachusetts government in its grip.

As the hostility between the Otises and the Hutchinsons intensified, the younger Otis soon saw an opportunity to defend the interests of his most important clientele, the merchants of Boston, and, at the same time, to make life difficult for the new Chief Justice of the Superior Court. His method was to challenge the legality of what were called general warrants, or writs of assistance. Officials used these warrants to enforce the Navigation Acts, parliamentary laws that required the colonists to pay duties on certain regulated goods. Because of efforts to avoid the payment of these duties, the acts engendered rampant smuggling. In response, the writs gave customs officers the unlimited right to search private houses, warehouses, and ships for smuggled goods, without having any particular knowledge that a crime had been committed. Much to the merchants' displeasure, any goods deemed contraband could be seized and sold by the government's agents. Because the writs needed to be renewed upon the ascension of a new monarch, George II's death in 1760 provided Jemmy with an opportunity to raise the question of the writs' validity.

The case came before the Superior Court in February 1761, with Thomas Hutchinson presiding. Otis's colleague, Oxenbridge Thacher, presented the substantive legal argument. Focusing on an obscure technical point, he challenged the exact legal form of the writs and contested the authority of the Massachusetts Superior Court to exercise what amounted to chancery court powers, which he said it did not have. Otis took another approach. He turned the case into a matter of constitutional principle rather than dry legal precedent. In a presentation lasting over four hours, Jemmy charged that the writs violated fundamental English liberties and were an affront to natural law. If general warrants were allowed, he said, no one would be secure against the arbitrary power of the state. "This writ," he insisted, "is against the fundamental principles of law. . . . A man who is quiet [should be] as secure in his house as a prince in his castle." Only specific warrants issued on the basis of particular information should be allowed (a point that was later incorporated into the fourth amendment to the U.S. Constitution). Warming to his own rhetoric, he urged the court to "demolish this monster of oppression, and . . . tear into rags this remnant of Starchamber Tyranny." Raising the stakes even further, Jemmy challenged the authority of Parliament to make laws that violated basic individual rights. The laws of nature, he said, guaranteed certain liberties that no human institutions could contravene.

Despite a bravura performance, Otis lost the case. In the process, however, he electrified his audience and spread his fame throughout Massachusetts. He was henceforth identified as a major leader of the colony's opposition party. But Otis did more. He permanently changed the way colonists thought about their relationship with England. While ideas of rebellion were far from anyone's—including Otis's—mind in 1761, he had framed the questions not in terms of legal technicalities, but in terms of higher laws and fundamental principles. For the first time, someone had raised the question of the constitutionality of parliamentary acts in the colonies. Many years later, Mercy Otis Warren, admittedly not an unbiased witness, claimed that with this case her brother had laid "the foundation of a revolution." John Adams, a somewhat more impartial observer, maintained, "Then and there the child Independence was born."

Beyond that, Otis had also painted Chief Justice Hutchinson into a difficult corner. In deciding against the merchants and for the King, he emerged as a royal stooge and a potential threat to the colonists' rights and privileges. After that time, many citizens reflexively identified him with the unjust and hated policies of the admiralty officials, and, in time, with British tyranny itself. On a more personal level, from the time of the Writs of Assistance case, the Otises' public battle against royal policies was inextricably linked with their own personal vendetta against Thomas Hutchinson.

In the next few years, Hutchinson, as the colony's lieutenant governor, faced off against not one but two Otises. In 1761 the citizenry of Boston showed their approval of Jemmy's handling of the Writs of Assistance case by electing him to the House of Representatives. He joined his father, who had been restored to his seat and to his position as Speaker of the House. Together they used whatever means at their disposal to voice opposition to royal policies in general and to Hutchinson in particular. They were especially effective in using the Boston newspapers to raise suspicions, spread rumors, and make accusations against the lieutenant governor and his allies. After his father received his long-awaited seat on the Governor's Council in 1762, the younger Otis took on an even greater leadership role in the lower house.

As Mercy was carrying her last child, political events in Massachusetts took a turn that would radically alter the whole political landscape. Britain, in an effort to centralize and systematize its administration of the colonies, unwittingly set off an imperial crisis. At the time, however, neither Mercy nor her relatives could have suspected that the end of the French and Indian War would usher in a whole new era of relations between the colonies and the mother country. The Treaty of Paris in 1763 effectively ended the century-long contest between European powers for dominance of North America. Britain emerged as the undisputed winner, gaining possession of the entire eastern half of the North American continent. Yet even after the war had ended, royal officials decided to keep ten thousand troops on the mainland, ostensibly to deter any future French threat and to subdue the Indians. If the move seemed prudent to the British, it appeared potentially threatening to the colonists. As Anglo-Americans, they were familiar with a long tradition of political theory that rejected the whole notion of a standing army in peacetime. Such an army, it was said, smacked of tyranny, representing an intimidating presence that could be turned against the civilian population to crush dissent.

Maintaining large numbers of troops also cost a lot of money. Perhaps the most significant new reality of the postwar era was the emergence of England's massive public debt. In order to win the French and Indian War, Britain had expended vast sums, much of it borrowed. The national debt had nearly doubled, reaching a figure of £147 million. After the war's end, the British minister, George Grenville, sought new sources of revenue. He realized that the English people, already heavily burdened, could not and would not pay more taxes, so he cast his eyes toward the colonies. The colonists had, after all, benefitted directly from the war while bearing little of its expense. As British citizens, they had a duty to assume some of the financial burden.

In 1764 and 1765, Grenville proposed, and Parliament passed, two new laws concerning the colonies. The first was the Revenue Act of 1764, also known as the Sugar Act. This statute superseded the Molasses Act of 1733, one of the navigation acts that had placed a prohibitively high duty on the foreign molasses used to make rum. Widespread violations of the act, however, meant that the law was essentially a dead letter, its enforcement costing more than customs receipts were bringing in. Under the Sugar Act, this was all supposed to change. The duty on foreign molasses was lowered from a steep 6 pence per gallon to a more realistic 3 pence per gallon. Stricter enforcement, including elaborate documentation requirements, harsher penalties for infractions, and the possibility of prosecution in the vice-admiralty courts, would guarantee that the new law would be more widely obeyed—and hence, that more revenue would be generated. However obnoxious the colonists found the tightening of trade provisions, what they found truly menacing was its language. The Sugar Act was designed specifically so "that a revenue be raised . . . for defraying the expences of defending, protecting, and securing [the American colonies]." It was, in other words, a tax, whose revenues would be used to support the odious standing army in North America.

The new law stunned the colonists. For over a century and a half, the colonies had been basically self-governing. Each colony had its own assembly, to which the people sent representatives of their own choosing. Before the French and Indian War, Parliament had exercised its authority over the colonies primarily through the Navigation Acts, laws designed to regulate international trade in a manner favorable to the mother country. At times London had requisitioned special funds from the colonists to support extraordinary wartime expenditures, but never before had Parliament directly imposed a tax on them. As a result, the colonists had come to believe that *only* their colonial assemblies had the right to tax them. The English, however, were under no such apprehensions. Parliament, officials insisted, exercised supreme authority over the entire realm. Just because the body had never exercised its right to tax the colonists did not mean it did not possess that right.

Quickly following on the heels of the Sugar Act was the even more problematic Stamp Act. Passed in March 1765, the new law imposed a sliding scale of taxes on various paper goods. The Crown would appoint specially authorized dealers to sell officially embossed (i.e., "stamped") paper in the colonies. All public documents had to be written or printed on this paper; those which were not would be subject to confiscation. Legal documents not written on the special paper would not be legally enforceable. The scope of the act was enormous: it encompassed everything from newspapers, pamphlets, and almanacs, to wills, deeds, bonds, and contracts. It even included college diplomas, playing cards, and dice. In addition, the tax was to be paid in hard currency, a commodity always in short supply in the colonies. As word of the "extraordinary act" reached America, it spread what Mercy called "a general alarm throughout the continent."

Leading the opposition to these new acts was Mercy's brother, James Otis. In the space of a little over one year, from the spring of 1764 to the summer 1765, he wrote four extremely influential pamphlets that probed the nature of representation, the extent of parliamentary authority, and the character of colonial autonomy. Jemmy was among the first to understand the full significance of the new legislation. On the face of it, the Sugar Act appeared to be just another customs regulation. Yet Otis saw from the beginning that the statute represented a troubling shift in British policy—no less than an attempt to tax the colonists without their consent.

Published soon after the passage of the Sugar Act and in anticipation of the Stamp Act, his *The Rights of the British Colonies Asserted and Proved* was a radical statement of colonial rights. Otis based his arguments on natural law as well as British tradition. "Every British subject born on the continent of America or in any other of the British dominions is . . . entitled to all the natural, essential, inherent, and inseparable rights of our fellow subjects in Britain." One of the most basic rights, he said, was that taxes could be levied on a people only "by their consent in person or by deputation." The colonists had no such representation in Parliament; thus Parliament had no right to tax them. Although he acknowledged the body's right to regulate trade, he rejected its right to pass any act for the purpose of generating revenue. He, like most colonists, drew no distinction between internal and external taxes. Anticipating the arguments of future revolutionaries, he asserted, "I can see no reason to doubt but that the imposition of taxes, whether on trade, or on land, or houses, on real or personal, fixed or floating property, in the colonies is absolutely irreconcilable with the rights of the colonists as British subjects and as men. For what one civil right is worth a rush after a man's property is subject to be taken from him without his consent? If a man is not his *own assessor* in person or by deputy, his liberty is gone or entirely at the mercy of others." Government authority ended, he claimed, where individual freedom began.

Yet Otis was far from advocating rebellion. He was absolutely loyal to England and proud to be part of the British empire. "Were these colonies left to themselves tomorrow," he wrote in 1765, "America would be a mere shambles of blood and confusion before little petty states could be settled. How many millions must perish in building up great empires? How many more must be ruined by their fall?" In subsequent pamphlets, Otis modified the radicalism of his initial effort. The colonists, he maintained, had no right to unilaterally disavow the laws of the realm. Fearing that the logic of resistance might lead to calls for revolution, he emphasized more emphatically the absolute nature of parliamentary supremacy. Although he questioned the justice of particular laws, he never doubted that "the power of Parliament is controllable but by themselves, and we must obey." Peaceful petitioning and quiet deliberation would more quickly convince England of an act's injustice than more overt acts of rebellion. The British system, Otis insisted, would not long tolerate the infringement of state authority on individual rights.

His more moderate efforts notwithstanding, Otis's pamphlets laid the foundations for a principled resistance to British policy. After his death, Mercy would accurately call her brother "the first American who with masterly precision investigated the rights and defended the liberties of his country." Through his words and deeds, Otis struggled to find a middle ground between absolute parliamentary sovereignty on one hand and complete personal freedom on the other. Less than a decade later, Otis's position would be completely untenable. Americans came to believe that defending their liberties necessitated an overthrow of parliamentary authority. But Otis's views persisted in other ways. A strong respect for individual rights as opposed to state power became the cornerstone of what is known as the liberal tradition in American history. "Liberal," in this context, refers not to a leftist political orientation, but a commitment to individual rights and civil liberties. Eventually, this tradition would be embodied in the U.S. Bill of Rights. But in the early 1760s, just a few individuals, led by James Otis, were articulating such sentiments.

Despite Otis's calls for peaceful resistance, violent protests against the Stamp Act erupted in various colonial cities in the Summer of 1765. In Massachusetts, a group of merchants and tradesmen calling themselves the Loyal Nine—later the Sons of Liberty—decided that the best course of action was to intimidate the stamp distributors into resigning their commissions. On the evening of August 14, 1765, a large crowd marched through the streets of Boston carrying an effigy of stamp distributor Andrew Oliver, who also happened to be Hutchinson's brother-in-law. After destroying a small building rumored to be the future site of the stamp office, they burned Oliver in effigy and attacked his home. Their tactics were effective: the commissioner resigned the next day.

On August 26, the mob gathered again. This time they turned their fury on Lieutenant Governor Hutchinson. Otis had written a series of newspaper articles in which he argued that Hutchinson, despite official demurrals to the contrary, had secretly supported the Stamp Act's passage. (He had not.) Armed and agitated, the angry crowd marched en masse to the official's home. Invading his elegant residence, they dismantled the house, timber by timber. They hacked apart his furniture, scattered his personal papers, and stole his cash, silver, and valuables. Hutchinson and his family barely escaped with their lives. Subsequently, Hutchinson never forgave the people of Massachusetts for what he called "the most barbarous outrage which ever was committed in America." When it suited their purposes, Americans had not hesitated to destroy private property for the sake of a principle. Far from being a controlled expression of political protest, the demonstration had turned into a riot, and the people remained unrepentant. As Mercy later put it in her *History of the American Revolution*, "Ample compensation was indeed afterwards made [to Hutchinson] for the loss of his property, [but] the strong prejudices against his political character were never eradicated."

The episode did make colonial leaders reassess their tactics. Realizing that their protests might backfire, leaders began to explore more diplomatic methods of expressing their dissatisfaction with British policy. Soon the Massachusetts assembly called for an intercolonial meeting to consider the colonists' common objections and the means of united opposition. In October 1765, twenty-seven delegates from nine colonies gathered in New York for that purpose. Acting with calm and deliberation, they passed strongly worded resolutions condemning the Stamp Act and rejecting Parliament's right to tax them. They sent petitions to the King, Lords, and Commons requesting the law's repeal. To put teeth into their words, they called for a universal boycott of trade to and from Great Britain. The people responded wholeheartedly to their leaders' call for action. The Stamp Act was set to go into effect on November 1, 1765. So unified were the colonists that the day came and went—and not a single stamp was sold. Some historians, including Mercy Otis Warren, later maintained that James Otis had originated the call for the Stamp Act Congress. Whether or not it was his idea, the meeting represented, as Mercy said, "the first congress ever convened in America by the united voice of the people, in order to justify their claims to the rights of Englishmen, and the privileges of the British constitution."

The colonists' strategy, especially the boycott, soon paid off. The financially strapped British merchants, who had done an enormous business in the colonies and extended large amounts of credit to their American customers, soon began to pressure Parliament to withdraw the act. In March 1766, the statute was repealed. Rejoicing in their apparent victory, the colonists now reaffirmed their unconditional loyalty to the mother country. "The people of every description manifested the strongest desire," noted Mercy in her *History of the American Revolution,* "that harmony might be reestablished between Great Britain and the colonies. Bonfires, illuminations, and all the usual expressions of popular satisfaction, were displayed on this joyful occasion." But, with the perspective of hindsight, Mercy also observed that this joy was "short-lived." At the same time it withdrew the Stamp Act, Parliament passed another law, asserting its right to pass statutes binding the colonies "in all cases whatsoever." To those who paid attention, the Declaratory Act seemed ominous. "Amidst the demonstrations of this lively gratitude, there were some who had sagacity enough to see, that the British ministry was not so much instigated by principles of equity, as impelled by necessity," Mercy said. "These [citizens] . . . felt more resentment for the manner, than obligation for the design, of this partial repeal; their opinion was fully justified by the subsequent conduct of administration."

Britain's "subsequent conduct" toward the colonies was not long in coming. The mother country still had as much need as ever for money. In June, Parliament passed the Revenue Act of 1767 and several other measures, which together became known as the Townshend Acts. Like the Stamp Act, the new laws were designed to generate revenue. One provision placed an "external tax" on goods imported to the colonies from Britain, including glass, lead, tea, paper, and paints. To insure stricter enforcement, an American Board of Customs Commissioners was created, to be headquartered in Boston. Adding insult to injury, the funds generated by the Townshend

Acts would be used to pay the salaries of royal officials in the colonies, making hated functionaries such as Thomas Hutchinson independent of the people. "There was no check left on the wanton exercise of power in the crown officers," commented Mercy, "however disposed they might be to abuse their trust."

The colonists immediately responded to the new threat to their liberties. Presumably because the Townshend Acts bore a passing resemblance to the Navigation Acts, whose legality was not in dispute, British officials had convinced themselves that Americans would accept the new taxes. But Americans had repeatedly objected to *all* forms of parliamentary taxation, whether levied internally or externally. As Mercy put it, "It was not the sum, but the principle that was contested; it manifestly appeared that this was only a financiering expedient to raise a revenue from the colonies by imperceptible taxes. . . . To do so by the secret modes of imposts and excises would ruin their trade, corrupt the morals of the people, and was more abhorrent in their eyes than a direct demand."

Primed for action, Massachusetts again led the resistance. James Otis joined with Samuel Adams, a charismatic leader of the opposition party, to pen a letter to be circulated to the other colonial legislatures. Adopted by the Massachusetts assembly in early 1768, the Circular Letter reiterated the principle of no taxation without representation, rejected the Crown's plan to pay the salaries of royal officials in the colonies, and called for a revival of the boycott against Britain. The assembly's actions produced outrage in London. Furious at the colonists' impudence, British officials condemned the Circular Letter and ordered the Massachusetts legislature to retract it. When the assembly refused to do so, by a celebrated vote of 92 to 17, the Crown demanded that all royal governors dissolve their assemblies rather than allow their legislatures to discuss the seditious document.

The events that followed convinced Mercy, and many others in Massachusetts, that Britain was indeed the enemy. As tensions mounted, Governor Francis Bernard called for two regiments of troops to be moved from the frontier and to be stationed in Boston. The soldiers were necessary, he said, to protect customs officials and to enforce the new revenue acts. Mercy, along with many other colonists, regarded the troops as an ominous sign. "The standing army," she said in her *History*, "is the most ready engine in the hand of despotism." Far from bringing peace, the coming of the troops heightened hostilities between the people and the royal government. Friction between soldiers and civilians led to violent clashes, which eventually culminated in the so-called Boston Massacre. But the trouble began long before the massacre. For Mercy, the troop's entry into Boston on October 1, 1768, represented a turning point in the colonies' relationship with England. "The American war may be dated from the hostile parade of this day," she wrote in her *History of the American Revolution*, "a day which marks with infamy the councils of Britain."

During these tumultuous years, the Warren home emerged as a center for the discussion of radical politics, a kind of salon for revolutionaries. The Warrens' fine, two and one-half story clapboard home in Plymouth, with double high chimneys outside, carved wood paneling inside, and a large entry hall featuring a grand staircase, had become a favorite stopover point for various lawyers and politicians on their way between Boston and Cape Cod. One of the most frequent visitors was a young attorney named John Adams. A friend of Mercy's brother James, Adams frequently passed through Plymouth on his way to attend court sessions in the area. As early as 1764, Adams had visited the Warrens; by 1767 they were fast friends. His cousin, Samuel Adams, also prevailed on the Warrens' hospitality. James Otis, Junior, of course, had more than one reason to visit, and he did so often.

With such a cast of characters passing under the same roof, discussions about politics were inevitable. A stay at the Warrens might entail a learned debate of the pros and cons of colonial representation in Parliament, a thorough dissection of Hutchinson's latest travesty against justice, or a review of possible methods of protest against the most recent British depredation. Years later, Mercy fondly remembered the times "by the Plymouth fire side, where many political plans originated and were discussed and digested." Among the plans purported to originate there were James Otis's plan for the Stamp Act Congress and the first proposals for the committees of correspondence, a letter-writing network that would link the towns and colonies throughout America. Whether the ideas actually emanated from discussions there or elsewhere, the Warrens' home clearly provided a forum where opponents of British policy could plot and strategize about the most effective means of resistance.

With her house as a political entrepôt, Mercy was never far removed from the political issues of the day. As she listened to the debates, she formed her own opinions. Privately, she could voice her views to all who passed under her roof. But she had not yet expressed her views publicly.

In the 1760s, while at the peak of her domestic responsibilities, Mercy began to make some exploratory efforts as a writer. At least three of her poems come from this era: "On Winter" from January 1759; "To J. Warren Esqr" from 1766; and "On the early death of two beautiful young ladies, Misses Eliza and Abigail Otis," also from 1766. It is likely that she wrote other poems during the period that either did not survive or are not dated. None of these early poems was published during Mercy's life, and none of them broached the touchy subject of politics, as do later poems. Consisting of four-line stanzas with a simple alternate-line rhyming pattern, the early poems contained certain themes—nature, death, God, and emotional longing—that would recur in her later, more complex and ambitious poetry. At first she was clearly testing her abilities and searching out the themes, ideas, and forms of expression on which she would build. Perhaps most significant, despite her other preoccupations and duties, she felt compelled to set down her ideas in verse: she was a writer by nature.

One of these early poems is noteworthy for what it foreshadowed about Mercy's attitude toward her husband's political career. By the mid-1760s, James Warren had taken his first steps into the political arena. After his father's death, he inherited his father's position as high sheriff of Plymouth, an office that was more honorary than functional. During the Stamp Act crisis, he assumed more substantial duties, becoming the co-author of Plymouth's protest against Britain's proposed taxation policy. The next year, Warren won election to the Massachusetts House of Representatives, a seat he would hold continuously until 1778. Eventually, his peers would acknowledge his leadership abilities and choose him Speaker of the House.

As natural, and even inevitable, as James's ascension to political prominence was, it is evident from Mercy's early poem that his new role troubled her. During his first term as representative in 1766, Mercy wrote a poem entitled "To J. Warren Esqr," subtitled, "An Invitation to retirement." In the poem she urged him to:

> Come leave the noisy smoky town
> Where vice and folly reign,
> The vain pursuits of busy men
> We wisely will disdain.

She lamented the tumultuous nature of the political process, where "warring passions" and "endless strife" were "the blackest source of pain." She reviled the politicians' efforts to court popular approval and urged her husband to return home, to a place she portrayed as a quiet haven:

> The solemn shades, the sylvan scene
> All natures bright array
> Secure and guard the wandering mind
> From errors baneful way.

Already she missed her husband and yearned for his return. She sought to lure him back from the corrupt world of politics so that he might resume his rightful place—by her side. In succeeding years, Mercy would grow even more impatient with the demands that the political world placed on her relationship with her husband.

* * *

In 1763, when she was thirty-five years old, Mercy Otis Warren had her portrait painted by the eminent artist John Singleton Copley. In the painting, Mercy appears much like other women of her social class. She is exquisitely but tastefully dressed, enveloped in the trappings of wealth—lace trimming, silk fabric, fashionable attire. She seems confident of her status, role, and position. But her image exudes something more: she is a woman in motion. Rather than posing seated, she is seen standing, one hand in midair. Her mouth is unsmiling, though not severe; she appears determined and composed. Her dark, serious eyes glance backward over her shoulder, as if the artist captured her just as she was about to leave the room.

In the 1760s Mercy *was* a woman in motion. She found herself the mistress of a busy and growing household. She was the mother of three sons and would soon bear two more. Her husband was a successful farmer and trader who was becoming increasingly prominent in provincial politics. But there was more that kept her on the move. Even at the height of her domestic responsibilities, Mercy continued to grow intellectually. She wrote poetry in her spare time. She listened and observed as her father, husband, brother, and others debated the complex questions of parliamentary sovereignty, political representation, and just resistance. She corresponded continuously with Jemmy and followed his tortured intellectual path as he grappled with the tension between individual rights and parliamentary supremacy. She experienced as her own his political successes and failures—first in his battle against the family enemy, Thomas Hutchinson, and then in his struggle against royal authority itself. No one, least of all Mercy, knew where events were headed. "There were few, if any, who indulged an idea of a final separation from Britain at so early a period; or that even wished for more than an equal participation of the privileges of the British constitution," she later wrote in her *History of the American Revolution.* For now, she sat on the sidelines. Soon, however, much sooner than anyone could have anticipated, she would be called upon to do much more.

CHAPTER THREE

Her Pen as a Sword

Just as the political crisis with Britain was deepening, tragedy struck the Otis family. In the early 1770s the elder James Otis became sickly. He retreated to his hometown of Barnstable, where he continued to exercise a local leadership role until he died in 1778. The end did not come so quickly for the younger James Otis. By the late 1760s, Jemmy had begun to slip in and out of insanity; in 1771 he had to be transported off to the Massachusetts countryside for a "rest." Although he lingered on for another twelve years, he never regained his position in Massachusetts politics. He had exited the political stage for good.

For a time, it looked as if the American Revolution itself would happen without the Otises. As her father and brother withdrew from the political realm, a most unlikely event occurred: Mercy Otis Warren stepped into the arena they had vacated. As a woman, she could not participate in politics in the same ways they had. Still, she found her own venue. With the advice and encouragement of her husband and various family friends, she began to write poems and plays with expressly political themes. Published under the cloak of anonymity, these works were satirical as well as poetic, caustic as well as humorous. They whipped up sentiment for the American cause and in effect, helped transform a petty, local squabble against Thomas Hutchinson into a fight against British tyranny. Sens-

ing both the need and the opportunity, Mercy took the remarkable step of picking up where her male relatives had left off.

* * *

As the 1760s passed into the 1770s, Mercy and her circle began to reassess their understanding of British intentions toward the North American colonies. Years later, Mercy would
chronicle the shift in her *History of the American Revolution,* using the themes of classical republicanism to express Americans' growing disenchantment with England. As she saw it,
the colonists initially gave Britain the benefit of the doubt.
England was, after all, the mother country. Strong common
ties of law, language, religion, and kinship linked the colonies
with Great Britain. The Stamp Act, Americans thought, reflected Britain's misunderstanding of the colonists' situation;
its repeal reaffirmed the desire for reconciliation and mutual
respect. Although some Americans began to grow wary of the
British government, they remained steadfastly loyal to the King,
whom they regarded as their ultimate protector and guardian.

But with the levying of new taxes and the garrisoning of
troops in Boston, British policy seemed to take on a more insidious design. Mercy viewed these actions through the lens of
assumptions and expectations garnered from her reading of
writers such as Niccolò Machiavelli, James Harrington,
Algernon Sidney, John Milton, John Locke, and John
Trenchard and Thomas Gordon. Diverse though they were,
these writers stressed certain common themes. Republican governments, they warned, were susceptible to degeneracy and
corruption. In England, corruption would express itself
through an imbalance between the King, Lords, and Commons. If one branch of government gained a disproportion-
ate share of power, the people would lose their rights and eventually be reduced to a condition of political slavery. Certain
changes signalled these tendencies, including the creation of
a standing army, the appointment of legislators to patronage
positions known as "places," and the undue influence of the

King's ministers on the legislative process. Only constant vigilance and the practice of civic virtue could protect the people from tyranny and preserve their freedom. As Mercy saw it, Americans, with their simplicity of manners, general equality of condition, and commitment to public morality, were ripe for self-government. They would not tolerate any infringements on their rights and liberties.

By the late 1760s and early 1770s, the new British policies convinced many colonists, including Mercy, that the King's ministers—though not the King himself—were engaged in "nothing less than a systematical plan of slavery designed against them." Political leaders in Massachusetts warned of a coming crisis. "We must exert ourselves to awaken our Country men to Sense of the danger they are in of immediate and perhaps irrecoverable Ruin," Samuel Adams told Mercy's husband in 1772. "Every kind of Opiate is administered daily which our Enemies can invent." Fearing the course of events, Mercy wrote in the next year to a friend, "What fatal infatuation has seized the parent state, that she is thus making illegal encroachments on her loyal subjects, and by every despotic measure urging these populous, brave, and extensive colonies, to a vigorous union in defence of their invaded rights." Only if these measures would cease, she said, "may [we] yet . . . prevent the sad alternative of either bowing beneath the *bands* of slavery or of repurchasing our plundered rights by the blood of the virtuous citizens." The colonists felt besieged and assaulted, increasingly alert to what appeared to be a comprehensive conspiracy against their liberties.

Mercy's fireside tutorials about rights and liberties took on added significance when it became clear that neither her father nor her brother could lead the fight against encroaching tyranny. By the 1770s, Colonel James was in his seventies and suffering from the disabilities of old age. As sentiment against England grew, he spent more of his time in Barnstable rather than Boston. Mercy's hometown was deeply divided over the prospect of war with England. Many citizens of the conservative backwater harbored doubts about the legality of the resistance movement and longed to remain loyal to the Crown. As a respected elder, Colonel Otis tried to mediate the conflict, nudging townspeople closer to revolution and at the same time not alienating those who were still sitting on the fence. Even under his leadership, the town voted down a call for immediate independence issued by the Massachusetts assembly in 1776. Eventually, Barnstable citizens did side with the patriots. However, not long after the formal break with England, Colonel Otis grew severely ill and died on November 9, 1778.

The plight of the younger Otis was more tragic. By the late 1760s, Jemmy began switching his political positions frequently and unpredictably. He also began to behave erratically, a trait no doubt exacerbated by his heavy drinking. In May 1768, he made a public spectacle of himself. During the assembly's final vote on the election of Thomas Hutchinson to the upper house, Otis dashed through the house chamber shouting that the choice was between "pensioner or no pensioner." Members reacted to Otis's breach of decorum with shock, repulsion, and dismay.

The effective end of Otis's leadership role came on the evening of September 5, 1769. Entering the British Coffee House in Boston, Otis encountered his bitter enemy, John Robinson. A member of the American Board of Customs Commissioners, Robinson was a symbol of Britain's hated taxation policies and the frequent object of Otis's vitriolic newspaper attacks. According to witnesses, Robinson, upon spying Otis, rushed up to him and grabbed him by the nose. Someone doused the lights. In the ensuing scuffle, Robinson apparently struck Otis numerous times with a heavy cane. When it was all over, Jemmy had incurred several deep cuts and a severe concussion. Immediately afterward, Mercy sent an impassioned letter to her brother, begging to know of his condition and of the circumstances surrounding the incident. "Is it possible," she wrote, "that we have men among us under the guise of officers of the Crown, who have become open assassins? Have they with a band of ruffians at their heels attacked a gentleman alone and unarmed with a design to take away his life?" Subsequently, Otis sued Robinson in a civil suit. The jury vindicated Otis, granting him £2,000 in damages. The wounded leader declined the monetary award. Instead he asked for, and received, a public apology from Robinson.

Otis, however, never really recovered from the attack. With his grasp on reality teetering, the assault sent him over the edge. It shook him emotionally as well as physically. Although he was later reelected to the assembly, he acted bizarrely—leaving rooms suddenly and for no apparent reason, shouting obscenities without provocation, and equivocating wildly in his political positions. In November 1771, he was declared *non compos mentis*. The following month Thomas Hutchinson recorded in his diary, with some vindictiveness, that Otis had been bound hand and foot and taken off to the countryside. The younger Otis lived with his father until the Colonel died, then with a family friend in Andover. In his saner moments, James returned to Boston, only to leave again quickly. "Your Brother Jem dined with us yesterday," Mercy's husband reported in 1775. "[He] behaved well till dinner, was almost done and then in the old way got up went off where I know not; has been about at Cambridge and Roxbury several days." In 1778, his collapse was complete: he was seen trading his law books for liquor. His death five years later was as dramatic as his life. On May 23, 1783, during a tremendous thunderstorm, he stood leaning against the front doorjamb of the house in Andover. A bolt of lightning struck the chimney. Travelling through the entire structure, the charge electrified the doorway and struck Jemmy dead.

Now, for the first time in decades, no male Otis held a leadership role in provincial politics. But the involvement of James Junior and Senior had a lasting impact—both on Massachusetts politics and on Mercy Otis Warren. Perhaps their most enduring legacy was the persistence of the family feud between the Otises and Thomas Hutchinson. Personally and politically,

Hutchinson obsessed the Otises. They were envious of his successes, fixated on the hope of his failure, preoccupied with hastening his downfall. Ironically, it was not so much the differences as the similarities between the two families that produced the tension. Hutchinson had what the Otises wanted, and he had it on a far grander scale. While the Otises were petty regional traders, Hutchinson's family had made a fortune in international commerce. At a time when Hutchinson held numerous government offices, the Otises occupied seats only in the lower house of the assembly. While Hutchinson commanded a vast network of influence on both sides of the Atlantic, stretching to the highest levels in England, the Otises, having failed to secure connections across the sea, reached down for support—to the citizenry of Massachusetts.

This is not to say that the rivalry between the Otises and Hutchinson was merely the result of envy. The persistence, intensity, and virulence of the conflict suggest that much more was at stake: at the most basic level, it was a struggle for status, wealth, and prestige; at another level, it reflected a conflict over the distribution of political power; but at the highest level, it was a deeply rooted controversy over constitutional principles. At a certain point the Otises's attacks on Hutchinson became an assault on the whole system of imperial government. Whatever the similarity in their aspirations, the Otises diverged from Hutchinson when it came to identifying the source of political danger. While Hutchinson attributed the problem to the people, the Otises saw Hutchinson himself as the threat. Using newspapers, other print media, and political organizing tactics, the Otises linked Hutchinson in the popular mind with the hostile policies implemented by Parliament. Both were portrayed as working toward the same insidious end: to deprive the people of their rights and privileges. To a large extent, the Otises were successful in their efforts; the name Hutchinson became anathema.

With the withdrawal of both male Otises from provincial politics, the feud seemed to have reached a natural conclusion. But then, an unexpected figure stepped in. Picking up where her brother and father left off, Mercy Otis Warren entered the political realm. If the male Otises could not bring Hutchinson down, Mercy would try. That she even attempted to do so was a testimony to her strength of character, her unorthodox education, and the unwavering support she received from the men around her. Whatever reservations she or others shared about women in politics, at that moment being an Otis took precedence over being a woman.

Her brother's encroaching insanity caused Mercy to consider an expanded political role for herself. By 1770, she sensed Jemmy slipping away from reality. In that year, she wrote a poem, not published during her lifetime, called "A Thought on the inestimable Blessing of Reason, occasioned by its privation to a friend of very superior talents and virtues." She celebrated rationality as the highest God-given talent: "A ray divine, let down from Heaven,/A spark struck from effulgent light." Tracing the disastrous effects of reason's decline, she observed that the demise of rationality would "level proud imperious man/With the least worm in nature's plan." Pained though she was, she tried to extract a lesson from her brother's deterioration: "From reason's laws let me ne'er swerve/But calmly, mistress of my mind/A friend to virtue and mankind." In the following years, Mercy watched her brother's continued dissolution with sadness and dismay. "It is indeed hard to submit calmly," she wrote to a friend in 1773, "to see those abilities which once equalled and even surpassed many of the first characters, clouded, shattered, and broken: to see the mind of a man so superior thus darkened, and that man a most affectionate brother, is grief beyond expression." From the ashes of Jemmy's life, however, she began to discern a new course of action for herself.

Gradually, Mercy began to assume some of her brother's functions, beginning first with his correspondence with the eminent British historian, Catharine Sawbridge Macaulay. The author of the multivolume *History of England from the Accession of James I to that of the Brunswick Line*, Macaulay had written to

James in 1768 to congratulate him on his defense of American rights. Over the years, the two had exchanged many mutually admiring letters discussing history, republican liberty, and the course of the British empire. As Jemmy's faculties declined, he no longer responded to Macaulay's inquiries. In June 1773, Mercy wrote to Macaulay to inform her of her brother's deteriorating mental state. But she did not leave it at that. Instead, she opened the possibility for an exchange between herself and the great historian, and Macaulay was receptive. From that time on they corresponded regularly, except for a long hiatus during the Revolutionary War.

The exchanges were important for Mercy in numerous ways. Macaulay provided a female role model for Mercy—one "whose elegant writings reflect so much lustre on her sex," as Mercy put it. Macaulay was neither intimidated by men nor apologetic about her work. She was an unabashed republican and vociferous in her beliefs. Mercy clearly admired her. The eagerness with which she initiated the correspondence indicates that Warren longed for a connection with a woman whose concerns took her far beyond the typical female world of children, family, and home. It suggests that Mercy herself harbored hopes for a broader role. But Macaulay also offered the American woman something else. For many years, Warren had neither the time, the opportunity, nor the forum in which to voice her political opinions. Through her exchange with the British historian, she found her first epistolary outlet for her pet theories about society, government, and human nature. Macaulay acted as a critical audience whose opinion Mercy respected. She not only helped Mercy refine her prose, she sharpened the American's vision of politics. After testing her ideas out on Macaulay, Mercy later incorporated many of the same concepts, often using the same words and phrases, into her *History of the American Revolution.*

The most obvious sign that Mercy had assumed her family's mantle was the fact that she now began to publish her political writings. The vendetta against Hutchinson more than any antagonism toward Britain drove her to this course of action.

While she could not participate directly in the day-to-day political scene, as her brother and father had, she used the only means at her disposal—her pen—to continue the battle.

A closely related series of events led to her first publication. After Governor Bernard departed for England in August 1769, Thomas Hutchinson was appointed to the post of acting governor. During this time, tensions between the Bostonians and the occupying British troops mounted. On March 5, 1770, a confrontation occurred between the King's soldiers and a raucous mob that had gathered outside the Customs House. Five unarmed citizens were killed. Horrified, the colonists labelled the event the "Boston Massacre" and charged that the episode represented confirmation of a comprehensive British plot against American liberties. Holding the acting governor responsible, citizens agitated to prevent Hutchinson from receiving the prize he had long sought, the royal governorship. But one year later, the news arrived: Hutchinson had received the appointment.

Mercy's first published work was a thinly disguised attack on Hutchinson. Issued anonymously, *The Adulateur* was a wickedly satirical play written in blank verse, presented in two installments in a Boston newspaper, the *Massachusetts Spy* of March and April 1772. Mercy set the action in the mythical, despotic kingdom of Servia, creating a cast of characters who represented thinly veiled caricatures of real-life political figures. Like many other patriots, Mercy saw a direct parallel between ancient history, especially that of republican Rome, and modern-day events. As a result, her characters had names that were either farcical in nature or drawn from classical antiquity: Rapatio represented the notorious Hutchinson; Limpet, Hutchinson's relative, Lieutenant Governor Andrew Oliver; Brutus, James Otis, Jr.; Rusticus, James Warren; and Hortensius, John Adams, among others.

Her point was simple: to warn citizens of the evil, insidious intentions of the new governor. Rapatio (Hutchinson), she said, was "a tool" surrounded by "fawning courtiers," who "cring'd and bow'd and fawn'd/To get a place." He would stop at nothing to achieve his personal ambitions, even if it meant destroying the people's liberties or taking their lives. Mercy had Rapatio say aloud the words that she suspected lay in Hutchinson's heart:

> Tho' from my youth ambition's path I trod,
> Suck'd the contagion from my mother's breast;
> The early taint has rankled in my veins;
> Dispotic rule my first, my sov'reign wish.
> Yet to succeed, beyond my sanguine hope,
> To quench the generous flame, the ardent love
> Of liberty in Servia's free born sons,
> Destroy their boasted rights, and mark them slaves:

In an episode meant to evoke the Boston Massacre, Rapatio ordered the killing of innocent civilians. One character challenged the others, "Tell me ye patriots/Will you submit to fall without a struggle?" Mercy framed the response using what she had learned from her brother. During the Writs of Assistance case, James Otis had proclaimed, "The only principles of public conduct that are worthy of a gentleman or a man," he said, "are to sacrifice estate, ease, health, and applause, and even life, to the sacred calls of his country. These manly sentiments, in private life, make the good citizen; in public life, the patriot and the hero." In the play, Mercy had Brutus, the James Otis stand-in, exhort the populace in the following terms:

> Rather let Servia tumble from her basis,
> And in one general ruin cover all,
> Than see her citizens oppress'd with chains
> And sweetly slumbr'ing in the gilded fetters.
> The man who boasts his freedom,
> Feels solid joy—tho' poor and low his state,
> He looks with pity on the *honor'd* slave.

Mercy ended her work with a warning about the future. The time might soon arrive, she said, when "murders, blood and carnage,/Shall crimson all these streets"—and when people might have to take up arms to defend their liberties. In one sense, Mercy's work, by attacking British tyranny and defending American rights, represented a logical extension of Jemmy's earlier ideas. But unlike her brother, who rejected the notion of armed conflict with Britain, Mercy did not shrink from the possibility of violent revolt.

That Mercy chose a play as her first medium of public political expression was significant. Unlike her brother, Mercy did not appeal to the public through political treatises, learned pamphlets, or scholarly dialogues. She chose a more literary genre. Yet plays were not commonplace in Mercy's world. Puritan Boston still regarded plays as scandalous and immoral, and prohibited public performances. Although she had read many plays, including works by Shakespeare and Molière, she probably had never seen a play performed on stage. It is not surprising, then, that considered as a play, *The Adulateur* fell short; it lacked a full-fledged plot, character development, and dramatic resolution. But as political satire, it was a masterpiece. As one literary critic put it, *The Adulateur* was "essentially a propaganda pamphlet, ideologically a piece with the other publications of the pre-revolutionary radical press. . . . [It] was more weapon than work of art." The dramatic genre also had other appeals, for she wanted to entertain as well as instruct her audience; she felt that the consideration of even serious issues could benefit from a lighter touch. In the introduction to her *Poems, Dramatic and Miscellaneous,* she wrote, "Theatrical amusements may, sometimes, have been prostituted to the purposes of vice; yet, in an age of taste and refinement, lessons of morality, and the consequences of deviation, may perhaps, be as successfully enforced from the stage, as by modes of instruction, less censured by the severe; while, at the same time, the exhibition of great historical events, opens a field of contemplation to the reflecting and philosophic mind." The lugubrious structure of *The Adulateur* suggests that Mercy did not intend for it to be performed on stage. Rather, she probably imagined people reading her sketches aloud to one another in drawing rooms, coffee houses, and taverns throughout the colony. She would express herself politically in a way that used her talents most effectively.

The impetus for the writing of her next play resulted from the publication of a correspondence between the nefarious Hutchinson and Thomas Whately, a former secretary to the Treasury under George Grenville. Writing informally and unofficially over the course of several years, Hutchinson had expressed a variety of doubts about the political situation in the colonies. He voiced grave disappointment over the inability of the Massachusetts executive to maintain control over the legislature. He predicted that Parliament would punish those who undermined the operations of the colonial government and reward those who supported it. He also suggested, among other things, that if the colonies' link with England were to be maintained "an abridgement of what is called English liberty" would probably be necessary. Though he had expressed such opinions before, the letters, when presented collectively, conveyed a sense that Hutchinson and other colonial officials were actively plotting with British officials to destroy American freedom.

Hutchinson, of course, never intended for the letters to become public knowledge. Secretly passed in England from a British official (probably former Massachusetts Governor Thomas Pownall) to Benjamin Franklin, they were then sent to the Speaker of the Massachusetts House, with strict instructions to circulate them privately but not to print them. Tradition has it that the letters were first read aloud in early 1773 at the Warren's house in Plymouth. As rumors of their explosive contents spread, pressure for publication built. Finally, in June 1773, newspapers throughout the colonies printed the documents. They exposed the treachery of Hutchinson and, by implication, the entire British government for all to see.

As if to add fuel to the fire, Mercy published *The Defeat* in the May 24 and July 19, 1773, issues of the *Boston Gazette*. Set once again in Servia, the play contained many of the same characters of the earlier play, including Rapatio (Hutchinson), Limpet (Oliver), and Honestus (James Bowdoin). Short and fragmentary in nature, with even less of a plot than *The Adulateur*, its purpose was to emphasize the gravity of Hutchinson's crimes and to compound his humiliation. Alluding to the publication of the Hutchinson-Whately letters, Honestus, one of the "Virtuous Senators," told Proteus that his leader's pretense has been stripped away. Echoing the classical republican themes of conspiracy and corruption, the character proclaimed,

> Go tell thy master he deceives no more
> The cover'd sting, the half disguis'd plan,
> Peeps through the veil, and shows the abject man,
> Who for a place, a grasp of shining earth,
> Has stab'd the vitals, that first *gave him birth.*

Hutchinson was one of the few native-born royal governors of the colonial era. As Mercy's work pointed out, however, his nativity did not deter him from betraying his fellow citizens. In a direct reference to one of the most chilling passages in the letters—Hutchinson's suggestion that an abridgement of British liberties in the colonies might be necessary, she had Limpet unsuccessfully argue his superior's case: "Twas deem'd impossible the just Rapatio/Should plead Necessity for an Abridgment/Of native Freedom to a British Race." The extent of Rapatio's (Hutchinson's) treachery was so great that even his subordinates could not believe it. As a whole, *The Defeat* articulated a sentiment that Mercy later expressed in her *History of the American Revolution*: Hutchinson was "the principal author of the sufferings of the unhappy Bostonians, previous to the convulsions which produced the revolution." Her father and brother had been right to identify him as the immediate source of the colonists' misery. Conveniently, Mercy's personal biases intersected with the larger political currents of the time.

Shortly thereafter, as if to confirm Mercy's view, Hutchinson proceeded to play a pivotal role in one of the most notorious episodes of the pre-revolutionary era. In March 1773, Parliament passed the Tea Act, a law designed to rescue the foundering British East India Company from bankruptcy. The statute allowed the company to sell its tea at a deep discount in the colonies. In addition, the company was given the right to select certain agents to sell the tea, giving those fortunate persons a monopoly on the sale of tea in America.

Unbeknownst to Parliament, the Tea Act violated numerous American sensibilities. Tea was a privileged article in colonial society. By the mid-eighteenth century, it was the hot beverage of choice and, for wealthy individuals, the focus of an elaborate ritual. Exotic brands of tea and exquisite silver objects announced the owners' social status. But less wealthy colonists consumed the beverage as well, less conspicuously but just as voraciously. Like sugar and chocolate for later generations, tea was, according to Mercy, "an article used by all ranks in America; a luxury of . . . universal consumption. . . . As by force of habit, this drug had become almost a necessary article of diet[.] The demand for teas in America was astonishingly great." Yet tea was politicized as well as popular. Under the terms of the Revenue Act of 1767, Parliament had placed a tax on all imported tea. Despite the law's repeal in 1770, England had retained the tea tax as a symbolic reminder of Parliament's ultimate authority. In retaliation for the new Tea Act, the colonists continued to boycott British tea and to purchase smuggled Dutch tea in great quantities.

On the face of it, the Tea Act benefitted the colonists by actually lowering the price of their favorite beverage. But the colonists did not regard the law as beneficent. Smugglers feared that the colonists might start buying the cheaper British tea in preference to the contraband Dutch tea. Those merchants who were not selected to sell the British tea naturally resented the monopoly of the chosen few consignees, a select circle that happened to include two of Thomas Hutchinson's own sons. Most of all, patriots feared that the colonists might be lured by the prospect of cheap tea into abandoning their principled boycott of British tea. Whatever Parliament's intentions, colonists regarded the act as an insidious effort to undermine their opposition to parliamentary taxation policies.

In response to the law, patriots throughout the colonies mobilized. In New York City and Philadelphia, colonists refused to allow the ships carrying the British East India tea to be unloaded; the ships eventually returned to England. In Charleston, South Carolina, the ships were unloaded but the tea remained unsold, locked in warehouses. Mobs in other towns simply refused to allow the ships to land. In Boston, however, Hutchinson hunkered down for a fight. He ordered that the ships carrying the tea be allowed to dock. At that point, a group of patriots, under the leadership of John Hancock, began an around-the-clock citizen patrol to prevent the tea from being unloaded. A stalemate ensued, but the patriots knew that Hutchinson had an ace-in-the-hole. On December 17, the legal period for payment of the tea tax would expire. As the leading royal official, Hutchinson would then have the authority to send in the British navy to confiscate the tea for non-payment of the required duty. One way or another, he believed he would get the tea into the colony.

On the night of December 16, the patriots trumped him. In the dark of night, about fifty men, dressed as Indians, boarded the three ships carrying the tea. With great dispatch, they dumped 340 chests of British East India tea, worth £9,000, into Boston Harbor. As Mercy described the incident in her *History of the American Revolution*, "a great number of persons, clad like the aborigines of the wilderness, with tomahawks in their hands, and clubs on their shoulders, . . . marched through

the streets with silent solemnity, and amidst innumerable spectators, proceeded to the wharves, boarded the ships, demanded
the keys, and with much deliberation knocked open the chests,
and emptied several thousand weight of the finest teas into
the ocean. No opposition was made, though surrounded by
the king's ships; all was silence and dismay."

In the euphoria that followed the Boston Tea Party, Mercy
weighed in with her pen. By this time, even though her works
had been published anonymously, she had acquired a literary
reputation among the close-knit circle of patriots and patriot-
sympathizers. Not one week after the Tea Party, when "the spirit
of liberty [was] very high," John Adams wrote to the Warrens,
"I wish to see a late glorious event celebrated by a certain poetical pen which has no equal that I know of in this country."
He proposed a scheme for the poem, to be set in mythical
times, involving a "frolic among the sea-nymphs and god-
desses." Mercy responded enthusiastically. Fleshing out
Adams's sketchy concept with imagination and daring, she
structured the poem as a debate between Neptune's rival wives,
Amphytrite and Salacia. As the two nymphs argued about the
relative merits of various teas, "the champions of the
Tuscararan race" (a reference to an Indian tribe, who symbol-
ized the disguised patriots of the Boston Tea Party) took matters into their own hands. The intruders

> Pour'd a profusion of delicious teas,
> Which, wafted by a soft favonian breeze,
> Supply'd the wat'ry deities, in spite
> Of all the rage of jealous Amphytrite.

The effect of the Indians' action was, according to Mercy, to
"bid defiance to the servile train,/The pimps and sycophants
of George's reign." In Mercy's poem, if not in reality, the Boston Tea Party vanquished England's evil designs. Mercy's
mythological rendering of the event delighted Adams. He
praised it as "one of the most incontestable evidences of real

genius which has yet been exhibited" and helped arrange for its publication in a Boston newspaper.

News of the Tea Party did not receive such a welcome reception in England. "This unexpected event," as Mercy noted in her *History of the American Revolution*, "struck the ministerial party with rage and astonishment." They were appalled by the colonists' wanton destruction of private property and horrified by their blatant scorn for English law. English leaders decided that it was necessary not only to punish the citizens of Massachusetts, but to isolate them from the other colonists, in order to prevent the spread of what historian Bernard Bailyn has called the "contagion of liberty." Parliament adopted four laws, known collectively as the Coercive Acts (in England) or Intolerable Acts (in America). Under the first law, the Boston Port Act, Boston Harbor would be closed to all traffic as of June 1, 1774; no ships could enter or leave the harbor until all the tea had been paid for. The second law, the Massachusetts Government Act, stifled a system of government that, according to Britain, nurtured dissent and resistance to imperial policies. The Governor's Council, which had previously been elected by the lower house (subject to the Governor's approval), was now to be appointed without the consultation of the lower house. These thirty-six *mandamus* councillors would hold office at the King's pleasure. Additional provisions limited the scope of town government and restricted the number of town meetings. "By this bill," as Mercy saw it, the "former charter [of Massachusetts] was entirely vacated." The Administration of Justice Act flew in the face of the colonists' objections to a standing army. At the governor's discretion, British officials, including soldiers and customs officials, could stand trial in England for alleged crimes committed in the colonies. Obviously, a change in venue would be more likely to produce a favorable verdict for the accused. Equally objectionable, the Quartering Act permitted the governor to commandeer unoccupied public buildings in which to house soldiers. The colonists could thus be forced to house the very agents of their subjugation. Colonists also considered a fifth law, the Quebec Act, as punitive, though it was not designed to be so. The law retained French governmental customs and procedures in the territory won from France after the recent war. In practice, this meant that in the Quebec province there would be no representative assembly, no trial by jury, and a state establishment of Roman Catholicism. Though not directed at British-Americans, the law terrified the colonists and seemed to foreshadow the day when they, too, would no longer enjoy traditional English rights and liberties.

On June 1, the Boston port shut down. People throughout the colonies solemnized the occasion with a day of fasting and prayer. Flags hung at half mast, muffled church bells pealed, shops closed. Once again, British officials had miscalculated the effect of their actions. The colonists greeted the sanctions with an "indignation" that Mercy called "truly inexpressible. It was frequently observed, that the only melioration of the present evils was, that the recal[l] of Mr. Hutchinson [that] accompanied the bills." Instead of isolating the offenders, people from the other colonies rallied behind the Bostonians and sent them food, money, and messages of moral support. Leaders throughout the continent began to agitate for an intercolonial meeting to discuss the prospects for a united resistance to British tyranny. The Boston Committee of Correspondence warned that if England could abrogate one colony's rights, it could—and would—do the same to the others. "You will be called upon to surrender your Rights, if ever they should succeed in their Attempts to suppress the Spirit of Liberty *here*. . . . *ALL* should be united in opposition to this violation of the Liberties of *ALL*." For many, the Coercive Acts represented the turning point in their affections toward England. As Mercy put it, "The people trembled for their liberties, the merchant for his interest, the tories for their places, the whigs for their country, and the virtuous for the manners of society."

The furor culminated in the First Continental Congress. Gathering in Philadelphia in September 1774, the delegates drew up a list of declarations expressing their opposition to British policy. But whereas they had previously petitioned the King, Lord, and Commons, this time they sent their objections only to the King, whom they regarded as their ultimate protector and last remaining link with England. Delegates also revived that most effective of weapons, the economic boycott. To enforce the boycott, Congress established the Continental Association. Not only were colonists asked to stop buying British goods, they were asked to make a public display of their commitment to the cause. The Congress requested that citizens jettison the superfluities of life and practice thriftiness, frugality, and self-sacrifice for the boycott's duration. Cardplaying, cockfighting, and horseracing were discouraged as frivolous. Elaborate funeral practices and mourning rituals, including the customary giving of scarves and gloves, were curtailed. The wearing of homespun (clothing) became a sign of patriotism. As Mercy later recounted in her *History of the American Revolution*, the people responded to the congressional initiatives with enthusiasm. Exaggerating perhaps only slightly, she observed, "History records no injunctions of men, that were more readily and universally obeyed, than were the recommendations of this revered body." For those who did not comply voluntarily, the local Committees of Safety enforced the provisions by identifying, warning, and ostracizing violators. Nonetheless, the rate of voluntary compliance with the boycott was remarkably high.

In years immediately prior to independence, both Warrens were at their peak period of activity and involvement in the American cause. James Warren had emerged as a significant figure in the resistance movement. Along with his duties in the Massachusetts assembly, in November 1772 he took on the responsibility of chairman of the Plymouth Committee of Correspondence. In May 1773, he was appointed to serve on the main intercolonial corresponding committee. In the wake of the Coercive Acts, he and Samuel Adams drafted a document, known as the Solemn League and Covenant, that called for immediate and rigorous economic sanctions against Britain as well as a boycott against those merchants or artisans who refused to sign the Covenant—in effect, a secondary boycott. Despite intense lobbying by the principal authors, many towns refused to adopt the Covenant, preferring instead to wait for the decrees of the Continental Congress to go into effect.

While James was caucusing and conspiring with other revolutionary leaders, Mercy was busy turning out more literary productions in the service of the cause. Mercy authored a poem, once again in a mythological vein, to spur support for the boycott. She listed the various items women must sacrifice, including "feathers, furs, rich sattins, and ducapes," "[the] finest muslins that fair India boasts, . . . Side boards of plate, and porcelain profuse," as well as the infamous tea ("choice herbage from Chinesan coasts"). Toward the end of the poem, she put in a pitch for her husband's Solemn League and Covenant. Virtuous Americans, she said, "leagu'd, in solemn covenant unite,/And by the manes of good Hampden plight, ... They'll fight for freedom, and for virtue bleed." In another poem, published in the *Boston Gazette* of February 13, 1775, she played on classical republican themes by contrasting the dissipation and corruption of the British ("Virtue turn'd pale, and freedom left the isle") with the industry and uprightness of the colonists ("They quitted plenty, luxury, and ease,/ Tempted the dangers of the frozen seas"). Despite the growing alienation between England and America, Mercy knew that a split would be wrenching, for, as she put it in the poem, "When civil discord cuts the friendly ties,/. . . social joy from every bosom flies." Through her literary productions, Mercy traced the painful process of disengagement.

Mercy soon returned to the genre that had served her so well before. On April 3, 1775, she published as a separate pamphlet *The Group*, a play satirizing the foibles, ambitions, and delusions of Boston's loyalist community and the new *mandamus* councillors. As in her earlier works, the play's strength lay in characterization rather than plot. In it she carried over some of the previous figures, such as Hazelrod (Peter Oliver), and added new ones whose ludicrous names told all: Brigadier Hateall (Timothy Ruggles), Sir Sparrow Spendall (Sir William Pepperell), Hum Humbug (Jonathan Erving), and Sylla (General Gage, the new royal governor). Short on dramatic action, *The Group* consisted primarily of a series of vignettes in which the main characters made speeches to one another. Bemoaning the colonists' unified response to the Coercive Acts, one loyalist character announced,

> Tho' proud Britain wafts her wooden walls
> O'er the broad waves—and plants them round these Coasts,
> Shuts up their Ports, and robs them of their bread,
> They're not dismay'd—nor servilely comply
> To pay the hunters of the Nabob shores
> Their high demand for India's pois'nous weed.

Despite Britain's depredations, the colonists had not relented in their principled resistance to England's unjust policies. The Coercive Acts had only served to unify them. Aware of the increasing possibility of bloodshed, in *The Group* Mercy predicted that the more virtuous patriots would triumph over their dissolute English masters. As Dupe, the loyalist Secretary of State, regretfully proclaimed,

> Their valour's great, and justice holds the scale
> They fight for freedom, while we stab the breast
> Of every man, who is her friend profest.
> They fight in virtue's ever sacred cause,
> While we tread on divine and human laws.
> Glory and victory, and lasting fame,
> Will crown their arms and bless each Hero's name!

Essentially a call to arms, the work helped colonists realize that active resistance was the logical consequence of their current position. Coming when it did, *The Group* solidified anti-British sentiment in and around Boston. In addition, it helped its author to gain wider exposure. Though she still published anonymously, Mercy had the gratification of seeing reprints of her text in the newspapers of New York City and Philadelphia. Eventually, it became her most popular and widely read pre-revolutionary work.

Mercy's desire for anonymity at this stage of her career was understandable. Political works published in newspapers at this time were often issued under pseudonyms or anonymously. Like other patriots, Mercy may have feared direct retribution by British officials or tory sympathizers, and she did not want to expose her home or family to danger. As she told James Winthrop in February 1775, he could do what he liked with her manuscript, but she did not wish to be named author "so long as the spirit of party runs so high." Anonymous publication probably also appealed to Mercy because she was a woman. A woman author might not be taken seriously on political subjects or might be chastised for having spoken on subjects outside the female purview. She wanted her work to be accepted on its own merits, without regard to the author's gender.

Anonymous publication, however, had its risks. Without Mercy's permission, another writer expanded the cast and broadened the plot of *The Adulateur* and issued it as a discrete pamphlet in 1773. In 1814, one Samuel Barrett claimed to be the author of *The Group*. Mercy, alarmed at the usurpation of one of her favorite works, asked John Adams to testify publicly to her authorship, which he obligingly did. In another case, she did not receive proper credit for many years for her influential tract against the Constitution, signed "A Columbian Patriot." Although she admitted to its authorship in a contemporaneous letter to Catharine Macaulay, not until the twentieth century did Mercy's descendant, the legal historian Charles

Warren, publicize the fact the she, and not Elbridge Gerry, was the true author.[1] Even today, the authorship of two pre-revolutionary plays sometimes attributed to Warren remains highly disputed. *The Blockheads: or The Affrighted Officers, a Farce*, from 1776, derided loyalist Bostonians, and *The Motley Assembly, a Farce*, published in 1779, chided moderate Americans whose sentiments for their country were wavering. Although the subject matter of both plays would have been congenial to Mercy, it seems unlikely that she wrote them. They differ from both her earlier and later plays in several ways: they are written in prose form rather than in blank verse; they are farces rather than satires; they lack classical settings and allusions; and they contain bawdy language and sexual innuendos that the dignified Mercy would almost certainly never have used in public. They also contain female characters, who are notably absent in her other pre-revolutionary plays. The fact that she did not lay public claim to them in later years, as she did with certain other pieces, reinforces the assertion that they were not hers—though the question of authorship does remain debatable.

Despite official anonymity, for those in the know, Mercy Otis Warren had become Boston's leading patriot muse. Yet all along, Mercy was ambivalent about her newfound vocation. She constantly struggled with the propriety of a woman writing about politics. At one level, she experienced the same self-consciousness and timidity of many first-time authors. She simply was not sure whether her work was good enough to stand up to public scrutiny. "I am sensible," she told her friend Hannah Winthrop, that "the world is already full of elegant productions, that entertain the imagination and refine the taste. . . . I would not willingly make an addition to the last

---

[1]See Mercy Otis Warren to Catharine Macaulay, December 18, 1787, Letterbook, 26, and Charles Warren, "The Federal Constitution in Massachusetts," *Proceedings*, Massachusetts Historical Society, 64 (Oct. 1930–June 1932), 143–64.

useless class, and dispairing of eminence in the first, I rather choose my manuscripts should be in the cabinets of my friends, to be perused when nothing more instructive or entertaining may offer."

Her fears went deeper. At this stage of her life, Mercy demonstrated a fairly conventional understanding of the relationship between the sexes. Although she believed men and women had equal intellectual capacities, she thought the two possessed inherently different natures. "Men nor women were not made to think alike—it cannot be," she wrote to Abigail Adams in 1807. While men were brave, warlike, and filled with "manly resolution," women were, in her view, delicate, weak, timid, and passive. The differences between men's and women's natures produced a separation in the tasks and duties that it was proper for each sex to undertake. Men belonged to the public realm; women to the private. Men, Mercy observed to Abigail, had "opportunities of gratifying their inquisitive humour to the utmost, in the great school of the world," whereas women, she said resignedly, "are confined to the narrow circle of domestic cares." Females must attend to their domestic tasks, if for no other reason than "perhaps for the sake of order in families." Even her own writing took second place to her other womanly duties. "Whatever delight we may have in the use of the pen, or however eager we may be in the pursuit of knowledge," she wrote to a young friend, ". . . yet heaven has so ordained the lot of female life that every literary attention, must give place to family avocations, and every page, except the sacred one, must be unfolded till all matters of oeconomy which belong to her department are promptly adjusted." A proper "methodical arrangement of time," she insisted, would produce the necessary leisure to engage in writing and other intellectual endeavors.

The separation of tasks extended to politics. Though there was little doubt that Mercy or other women could hold perfectly sensible political opinions, they were not supposed to seek out any political role. Nor should they speak or write pub-

licly about politics. Violating these accepted norms could lead
to disaster. The very act of engaging in politics was thought to
make women behave like men, resulting in the loss of their
feminine character and diminution of their distinctive feminine traits, such as delicacy, modesty, and restraint. In an essay
attacking the British feminist Mary Wollstonecraft, Timothy
Dwight argued that women who wanted political rights "voluntarily relinquish the character and rights of women. Women,
as such, have rights to tenderness, delicate treatment, and refined consideration. Men have no such rights. When women
leave their character, and assume the character and rights of
men, they relinquish their own rights, and are to be regarded
and treated, as men." In his post-revolutionary lectures on the
law, James Wilson maintained that although history had proven
that certain women, including Elizabeth of England, Zenobia,
Queen of the East, and Semiramis of Nineveh, could reign as
well as any male ruler, such women, he insisted, "had too much
of the masculine in them." Despite their successes, "in all of
them, we feel and we regret the loss of the lovely and accomplished woman: and let me assure you, that, in the estimation
of our sex, the loss of the lovely and accomplished woman is
irreparable, even when she is lost in the queen." Women, in
other words, should leave politics to men.

In light of these ideas, it was understandable that Mercy
experienced a certain amount of anxiety and ambivalence as
she began her career as a political writer. In venturing into
the political realm, she crossed an invisible boundary between
the sexes. In the 1770s, she voiced her political opinions ten-
tatively, only when specifically requested to do so. "Your asking my opinion on so momentous a point as the form of *government which ought to be preferred*," she told John Adams, ". . .
may be designed to ridicule the sex for paying any attention
to political matters. Yet I shall venture to give you a serious
reply." Highly sensitive to reproach, she bristled at any suggestion that she had overstepped the bounds of propriety. "I beg
pardon for touching on war, politicks, or anything relative

thereto, as I think you gave me a hint," she told Adams in another letter, "not to approach the verge of any thing so far beyond the line of my sex." Yet even as she became increasingly politicized, she proclaimed a willingness to resume the traditional female role. In her poem "On Primitive Simplicity," probably written in October 1779, she asserted,

> Critics may censure, but if candour frowns,
> I'll quit the pen, and keep within the bounds,
> The narrow bounds, prescrib'd to female life,
> The gentle mistress, and the prudent wife:
> Maternal precepts, drawn from sacred truth,
> Shall warm the bosom of the list'ning youth;
> While the kind mother acts her little part,
> And stamps the tablet on the infant heart,
> Each fervent wish, I to my country lend,
> And thus subscribe, the patriot's faithful friend.

While she found the proper bounds of female life to be "narrow," she claimed that she was willing to "quit the pen" and return to her role as mother. Both roles, she implied, had a political dimension, in being "the patriot's faithful friend." Proper lady that she was, Mercy did not want "candour" to "frown" on her behavior. She did not seek to affront the status quo between the sexes.

Ultimately, then, Mercy did not venture into the political realm primarily because she believed it was her right, but because the men in her life allowed her to do so. Beginning in the early 1770s, men encouraged her to write and publish for a larger audience, beginning with John Adams's idea for a poem on the Boston Tea Party. After she had produced "The Squabble of the Sea Nymphs," he set about arranging for its publication and dissemination. *The Group* was composed at the "particular desire" of her husband, who then sent the play to Adams. Once again impressed by the quality of Mercy's poetical "genius," he arranged for its printing in Philadelphia, where he was living at the time. Dr. James Winthrop, her friend's husband, asked Mercy to write a poem on the items that women would refuse to buy from England during the boycott following passage of the Coercive Acts. An unnamed "patriotic gentleman," who presented her with a blank book, requested a poem to be written therein on the importance of "primitive simplicity" among the revolutionaries. Only with the permission of her male mentors was Mercy able to overstep the "narrow bounds" of female life.

Yet these men supported her not because they believed in the equality of the sexes, but out of a combination of awe and self-interest. Recognizing that she possessed an extraordinary literary ability, they thought they could use her talents to further the patriot cause. "God has given you great abilities," James Warren wrote Mercy. "You have improved them in great Acquirements. . . . They are all now to be called into action for the good of Mankind, for the good of your friends, for the promotion of Virtue and Patriotism." Even her husband characterized Mercy as possessing "a Masculine Genius." Mercy's exceptional abilities gave her a special dispensation to speak about political matters. John Adams denied having suggested in a previous letter to Mercy that military and political ideas were "beyond the Line of her Sex." Contradicting himself somewhat, he then admitted that even if he did hold this view, he "should certainly think that Marcia [Mercy] and Portia [Abigail], ought to be Exceptions." Though ordinary women might still be expected to keep silent about political affairs, an occasional female genius could be tolerated—particularly when she did what men told her to do.

Yet even at this early date in her career, Mercy was not entirely acquiescent in her view of politics as an exclusively male preserve. Her pre-revolutionary writings reflected a basic confusion, or ambivalence, about women's proper role. "When the observations are just and honorary to the heart and character," she wrote to Catharine Macaulay, "I think it very immaterial whether they flow from female lips in the soft whisper of private friendship or whether thundered in the Senate in the bolder language of the other sex." Of course, Mercy no longer confined her observations to the "soft whisper of private friend-ship"; she was now asserting them in public forums. She de-fended her decision to write about political matters to her friend Hannah Lincoln, saying, "As every domestic enjoyment depends on the decision of the mighty contest, who can be an unconcerned silent spectator? Not surely the fond mother or the affectionate wife, who trembles lest her dearest connec-tions should fall victims of lawless power?" Because women had as much a stake in the outcome of wars or the conse-quences of debates in the statehouse as men, they could jus-tify expressing their own political opinions.

At this point in her career, Mercy was struggling to articu-late the proper relationship of women to the political process. A comparison of her depiction of women in her early poems as opposed to her plays highlights her ambivalence. Drawing on a classical republican trope, the early plays portrayed pa-triotism as a strictly male virtue. Neither *The Adulateur* nor *The Defeat* nor *The Group* revealed any signs of having been written by a woman. The authorial voice was not gendered, and male characters predominated. Full citizenship depended on the individual's willingness to take up arms in defense of his liber-ties. "These are sentiments," said Cassius in *The Adulateur*, "Which make us men." In fact, Mercy introduced only one female character in all of her pre-revolutionary plays (exclud-ing the two disputed plays). Called simply a "Lady," the figure emerged in an epilogue to *The Group*, in the characteristically feminine role of mourning the fate of the men going off to war. In Mercy's early plays, then, women were either absent altogether or made only a minimal contribution to the pol-ity—even then they did so only in the conventional role of passive observer.

In contrast to the plays, the revolutionary-era poems de-picted a broader, more energetic political role for women. In "The Squabble of the Sea Nymphs," she highlighted the influ-ence of females over men in boycotting tea:

> For females have their influence o'er kings,
> Nor wives, nor mistresses, were useless things,
> Ev'n to the gods of ancient Homer's page;
> Then sure, in this polite and polish'd age,
> None will neglect the sex's sage advice,
> When they engage in any point so nice,
> As to forbid the choice nectareus sip,
> And offer bohea to the rosy lip.

Men, Mercy implied, would ignore women's political opinions at their own peril. Similarly, she believed that the effectiveness of the nonimportation agreements depended on the voluntary compliance of women. In the poem written for Dr. Winthrop, Mercy listed a huge array of goods that women must sacrifice for the sake of the boycott. By "quit[ting] the useless vanities of life," women would make it possible "at once to end the great politic strife." Their actions would determine the movement's success or failure: "Thanks to the sex, by heavenly hand design'd,/Either to bless, or ruin all mankind." In the early poems, then, women were portrayed as having a dynamic and active role in the resistance movement.

It seems no accident that Mercy's vision of women's political involvement differed significantly according to the literary genre she used. This difference reflected an unresolved contradiction in Mercy's understanding of woman's role. Because her own ideas were unclear, she could not reconcile or integrate her understanding of female patriotism into a dramatic vehicle. She could not envision a political heroine whose activities drove the action of an entire play. Moreover, because she conceived of political participation in the narrow, classical republican sense, which required a resort to arms and direct political participation, she relegated women to a more subordinate role; they remained behind the scenes in her plays, as they did in real life. Unlike the plays, however, Mercy's early poems reflected an author who was groping toward another conception of women's role. "The Squabble of the Sea Nymphs," "To the Hon. J. Winthrop, Esq.," and "On Primitive

Simplicity" all suggested that women, even in their traditional roles as wives and mothers, exercised a profound influence on men, and hence, indirectly on the political process. In their role as consumers, women had a more obvious impact; their cooperation determined the success or failure of the boycotts against Britain. Tentative though they were, Mercy's early poems represented an effort to articulate a more expansive conception of women's contributions to the polity. Yet at this point in her career, Mercy's ideas were still paradoxical, if not self-contradictory.

* * *

Time would heighten the contradictions in Mercy's position. How could she, as a female author who was herself making a vital contribution to the revolutionary cause, regard patriotism as an inherently male attribute? How could she, who expressed the patriot position more capably than most men, believe that political participation was beyond the acceptable bounds of behavior for her sex? How could she, who saw that women made as many sacrifices for the cause as men had, maintain that citizenship was strictly a male preserve? In succeeding years, Mercy would grapple more directly with these issues. For now, she was too busy doing her work—as a propagandist of the patriot resistance—to develop a rationale for what she was doing as a woman.

CHAPTER FOUR

War Widows

As resistance became revolution, Mercy confronted the sobering realities of war. She feared for her own safety, and for the safety of her husband and children. More and more often, she felt abandoned, as James attended to the busy demands of a government at war. To her dismay, she found herself raising the children and tending the farm on her own. Unlike her friend Abigail Adams, she was not especially adept at managing the estate or making the best of adverse economic circumstances. She never really adjusted to her husband's absences; she missed him frequently and vocally.

Nevertheless, the war proved to be an important force in strengthening Mercy's character, most especially, her identity as a woman. Building on her previous literary efforts, she continued to write political poems and plays and to begin work on her magnum opus, a *History of the American Revolution*. She also turned toward her female friends for solace. The war reinforced her ties with other war widows, women whose husbands were away fighting the British or serving in a legislative or diplomatic capacity. Her lifelong (though sometimes strained) relationship with Abigail Adams was one result. But Mercy's influence extended to many other women as well. As the focal point of a far-flung epistolary network, she not only gave and received comfort, but dispensed that most sought-after of all commodities—information about the war and politics, about which she among women had a unique knowledge. Through the war, Mercy and her friends experienced what historian Lynn Hunt has called, in the context of the French Revolution, "the politicization of the everyday." Through their correspondence, the women came to a growing recognition of their own contribution to the patriot cause.

* * *

As late as 1775, many colonists remained reluctant to make the final break with Britain. Americans continued to see themselves as part of the English family. As Mercy put it, "Great Britain the revered parent, and America the dutiful child, had long been bound together by interest, by a sameness of habits, manners, religion, laws, and government." More than just a metaphor, the family imagery reflected a depth of feeling that made it difficult for colonists to contemplate the prospect of armed revolt. "Home, the seat of happiness, the retreat to all the felicities of the human mind, is too intimately associated with the best feelings of the heart, to renounce without pain, whether applied to the natural or the political parent," Mercy said. "There were few who did not ardently wish some friendly intervention might yet prevent a rupture, which probably might shake the empire of Britain, and waste the inhabitants on both sides of the Atlantic."

As Mercy and others saw it, however, Britain's continuing attacks on American liberty forced the colonists to take action. In April 1775, British troops marched to destroy munitions depots in rural Massachusetts; the bloodshed at Lexington and Concord created a further breech between England and America. Discussing the events in her *History of the American Revolution*, Mercy wrote, "The footsteps of the most remorseless nations have seldom been marked with more rancorous and ferocious rage, than may be traced in the transactions of this day. . . . A scene like this had never before been exhibited on her peaceful plains; and the manner in which it was executed, will leave an indelible stain on a nation, long famed for their courage, humanity, and honor." In November, the King declared the colonies to be in a state of rebellion and sent twenty thousand troops—including the notorious Hessians, German mercenaries hired by the British Government—to put down the revolt.

Yet because they sensed that they did not yet have the full support of the American people, delegates to the Continental Congress refrained from declaring independence. It took the publication of Thomas Paine's *Common Sense* in January 1776 to convince the majority of colonists that the time for separation had indeed arrived. A former corset maker and excise collector, Paine had recently emigrated from England to Philadelphia. Insinuating himself into radical political circles, he had become an ardent critic of British policy in America. In his famous pamphlet, Paine made the case for immediate independence from Britain. He attacked the colonists' last remaining link with England, King George III. Invoking the familial imagery that the colonists knew so well, Paine insisted that Britain was no longer acting as a good parent, for "Even brutes do not devour their young, nor savages make war upon their families." The problem lay neither with Parliament nor with the King's ministers; it was with the institution of hereditary monarchy itself. "For all men being originally equals," he asserted, "no *one* by *birth* could have a right to set up his own family in perpetual preference to all others for ever." In America, he proclaimed, "THE LAW IS KING. For as in absolute governments the King is law, so in free countries the law ought to be King; and there ought to be no other."

Common Sense sold over 100,000 copies, which would make it a bestseller even today. But at a time when America's population was only about 2.5 million, the work's impact and diffusion was phenomenal. As more people read the tract, they encouraged others to peruse it as well. Hannah Winthrop mentioned the "celebrated Pamphlet" in a letter to Mercy Warren, who, after digesting it, sent it on to Massachusetts politician James Bowdoin. Those who could not read it themselves probably heard it read aloud in local taverns or coffeehouses.

Part of the genius of Paine's work was that it was written in language that ordinary Americans could understand. His references and allusions were not to obscure Greek and Latin texts, but to the one work with which all colonists would be familiar—the Bible. Paine's prose also inspired. His flowing rhetoric assured Americans their cause was just. "Every thing that is right or natural pleads for separation," he asserted. "The blood of the slain, the weeping voice of nature cries, 'TIS TIME TO PART. Even the distance at which the Almighty hath placed England and America, is a strong and natural proof, that the authority of the one, over the other, was never the design of Heaven." Paine's pamphlet convinced many people who had been wavering or indecisive to forge ahead with the American experiment.

Sensing the emerging consensus, in July 1776 Congress took the final steps toward independence. Echoing Paine, Mercy wrote to Catharine Macaulay, "Thus Nature has furnished the continent with materials, and Providence has led [the country] to independence before her Children were conscious of their maturity." Drawing on the typical familial imagery, Samuel Adams told James Warren, "The Child Independence is now struggling for Birth. I trust that in a short time it will be brought forth." Soon it was.

The path to independence, however, placed tremendous demands on those leading the emerging nation. Mercy 's husband spent more and more time consumed with public business. After the passage of the Coercive Acts, James was elected President of the First Provincial Congress, the body that replaced the Massachusetts assembly. In 1775, he was elected Speaker of the House. When actual fighting began, he was appointed the Second Major General of the Massachusetts militia. In 1777, the Continental Congress named him a member of the three-man Navy Board of the Eastern Department, a job that involved purchasing supplies, disciplining officers, and supervising the creation of an American navy. Like many other overextended patriots, Warren held all of these positions simultaneously.

The beginning of armed resistance brought new dangers to the Warrens. After the clashes at Lexington and Concord, rumors swept through the colony reporting the savage behavior of the British soldiers—"Bloody ruffians," her friend Hannah Winthrop called them, who possessed "the ferocity of Barbarians." Mercy herself revealed that she had met a gentleman "who [had] conversed with the brother of a woman [who had been] cut in pieces in her bed with her new born infant by her side." Whether or not the rumors were true, they brought home the brutally terrifying realities of war.

Back in Plymouth, the Warrens' political sympathies put the family in potential danger. Deeply divided between Tory sympathizers and patriots, the town was riven with an "animosity and bitterness of spirit" that, according to Mercy, made "the restoration of harmony" nearly impossible. Each group threatened the other with bodily harm. In the summer and autumn of 1775, she and her children left the town several times, seeking refuge in patriot strongholds at Taunton and Watertown. At Watertown, she could also be with her husband, who resided there while the assembly was in session. During one of these visits, she met the General and Mrs. Washington, an experience that deeply impressed her and reaffirmed her faith in the American cause.

When she returned to Plymouth, she had her hands full: taking care of her sons; maintaining the house in town; and overseeing the Eel River farm. While she did have the assistance of servants, she felt the anxious burden of her responsibilities. She was not especially good at managing the business side of the family's affairs. Most important, she missed her husband sorely and ached for his return. "I know not how it is," she wrote to James, "but in your absence the sun seldom shines, Either Literally or Metaphorically."

What helped make the separations more tolerable was the support she received from an extensive network of female friends. Her closest friends were local women whom she had known for years, especially Ellen Lothrop, wife of a Plymouth doctor who lived right across the street from the Warrens, and Hannah Winthrop, wife of James Winthrop, a professor of Natural Philosophy and Mathematics at Harvard. This network of support also included relatives, such as her brother James's grown daughters, Sally Sever and Elizabeth Brown. The war extended Mercy's circle to encompass new acquaintances, such as the wives of other patriot leaders, including Martha Washington and Abigail Adams. Frequent letters as well as occasional visits kept the friends in close touch with one another.

As with most women of her generation, Mercy depended on her female friends for companionship, information, and support. But through her vast reading, Mercy had formed an elevated notion of friendship, a concept she called "rational friendship." "What is it that enlivens the social hour," she wrote to a young woman, "but a reciprocal esteem and a similarity of sentiment? And when that esteem is so well grounded as to give hope that it will not end with the flying hours, but be perfected, when time is no more, in the presence of him who is the fountain from whence flows benevolent affection, this and this only may be styled a rational friendship, and when founded on such a basis, nor clouds nor absence will prevent its completion." Such friendships endured beyond the grave. "If we may set our affections on any thing below the stars," she wrote to Hannah Winthrop, "we shall surely find indulgence for our fond attachments to friends, whose rational and reciprocal affection, we have no reason to think will terminate with time." Beyond entertainment, these friendships reaffirmed the social order and reflected the greater glory of God.

Of course, not all friendships attained this sublime level of commitment and concern. In choosing her own friends, Mercy seems to have distinguished between ordinary and extraordinary women. On the one hand, exceptional women such as Catharine Macaulay possessed "a commanding Genius and Brilliance of thought." She was a lady, Mercy told her son, "whose resources of knowledge seem to be almost inexhaustible." Most women did not measure up to such exacting standards. By contrast, General Putnam's wife, Mercy remarked, was "what is Commonly called a very Good kind of Woman, and Commands Esteem without the Graces of politeness, the Briliancy of Wit, or the Merits of peculiar Understanding above the Rest of her Sex." Yet such a woman had her strengths. She should "be Valued," Mercy insisted, "for an Honest, unornamented, plain hearted friendship Discovered in her Deportment at the first acquaintance." Other women had other virtues. "Sweetness of temper, gentleness of manners, an habitual serenity of mind, and the uniform practice of the social virtues," she told her daughter-in-law, "often compensate for the want of briliant talents or a scientific education." Thus even ordinary women could command respect and admiration. Though a bit of an intellectual snob, Mercy enjoyed friendships with a wide variety of women.

And the women valued Mercy's friendship. With their husbands away, they were left alone to manage the family farms or businesses, acting as "deputy husbands," to use historian Laurel Ulrich's term. These new tasks both challenged and frightened them. They sometimes doubted their abilities or felt overwhelmed by their new responsibilities. "The most Forlorn and Dismal of all States is that of widowhood," observed Abigail Adams to Mercy. But "how often does my Heart bleed at thinking how nearly my own Situation is allied to that, nor can I sometimes refrain from wishing that the wisdom of the continent had made choice of some person whose seperation from his partner would have been little or no pain, or mortification." Through their correspondence with one another, the women sustained each other's patriotism. "Your Faith that the united Efforts will be Blest with Success animates me," commented Hannah Winthrop to Mercy. "I catch a spark of that heavenly Flame which invigorates your breast knowing your Faith has a permanent Foundation and your acquaintance with those in the Cabinet must enable you to form a better Judgment than those who have not those advantages." The burdens felt lighter once they were shared.

Mercy also provided important information to her female correspondents. Women of the revolutionary era found themselves in a discomfiting situation. Although politics was considered a male affair, they knew that as the wives and mothers of politicians and soldiers they, too, had a stake in what happened in the political realm. Eagerly they sought out reports of the latest occurrences in the assembly halls, battlefields, and diplomatic chambers. In this situation, Mercy's access to patriot leaders and her skills as a political writer made her a highly regarded source. Dropping the customary female reticence about discussing political matters, women eagerly pressed her for news about the war and the rapidly changing political situation. She accommodated them as best she could. "Pardon my touching on a subject so much out of the road of female attention as the contents of this must be," Mercy wrote to Hannah Lincoln in 1774, "if I comply with your repeated requests I give you my sentiments concerning the present unhappy situation of my country." "I write in a very great hurry," she told Abigail Adams, "or I should touch a little on politicks, knowing you love a little seasoning of that nature in every production." The events of the day eroded the strict separation between public and private spheres. Because politics so directly affected their fates, women could be excused for probing into a traditionally male realm.

Besides providing information, the exchanges helped to politicize the female population. During the revolutionary era, some women engaged in very public displays of patriotic activity. In Massachusetts they signed the Solemn League and Covenant drafted by Mercy's husband; in Philadelphia they collected funds to support the Continental Army. In 1767, three hundred Boston women signed their own nonimportation agreement. A group of about one hundred women, appalled at the extortionate prices being charged by a Boston merchant for coffee, formed a mob outside of his warehouse and demanded that he turn over the keys to them—which he did.

Most women, however, endured more personal sufferings and made more private contributions to the cause. Staying at home, spinning homespun, or refusing to buy British tea represented key elements in the resistance movement, without which the boycotts would have failed. Sending one's husband's to Congress or the state assembly involved untold personal sacrifices for women. But when resistance became armed revolution, women were asked to make the hardest sacrifice of all: to allow their husbands and sons to go off to war. Through their correspondence, women began to see the significance of their efforts and to regard themselves as patriots. They saw that their contributions at home were as important to the war effort as their husbands' endeavors on the battlefield or in the statehouse. "I have the vanity," admitted Mary Fish of Connecticut, "to think I have in some measure acted the *heroine* as well as my dear Husband the Hero." The epistolary exchanges both reflected women's increasing politicization and stimulated the process further.

Mercy's correspondence also enabled her to form a friendship that would play a recurrent role in the course of her life. This was her friendship with Abigail Adams. Mercy had become acquainted with John Adams long before she met his wife. When John began to visit the Warrens in the mid-1760s, he and James Warren had come to be close friends and political allies. Mercy and Abigail, however, did not meet until July 1773, when Abigail, venturing from her Braintree home, visited Mercy in Plymouth. From the beginning, Abigail looked up to Mercy and deferred to her judgment. Nearly sixteen years younger than her friend, Abigail was largely self-taught, whereas Mercy obviously had enjoyed a more formal education. By 1773, Mercy had also acquired the beginnings of a literary reputation. As a result, Abigail often sought her friend's opinion on political matters, asked her advice about domestic affairs, and even attempted to imitate Mercy's rather convoluted prose style.

The friendship between Abigail and Mercy reveals a fascinating contrast between the lives of two highly intelligent and somewhat unconventional women of the revolutionary era. Despite the age gap, an immediate rapport sprang up between them. Sharing a mutual interest in politics and their travails as war widows, they initiated a frequent correspondence. In keeping with the patriot vogue for invoking ancient republican virtues and styles, they addressed each other with classical names: Mercy became "Marcia," after the wife of the Roman Republican orator Hortensius. Abigail became "Portia," after Brutus's wife, who swallowed hot coals upon learning of the death of her husband. Through their letters, the women also conveyed their literary predilections and tastes (Mercy liked Moliere, Abigail did not), transmitted the latest political news and gossip (Abigail particularly enjoyed Mercy's characterizations of public figures), and—important in a time of scarcity—exchanged cloth and other goods with each other, including French cotton, Irish linen, cambrick, shoe binding, and thread. Mercy, in fact, acted as an agent for Abigail, selling goods for her in Plymouth.

Naturally, the two friends also spent much of their time consoling one another over the absence of their husbands. "I find I am obliged to summon all my patriotism to feel willing to part with him again," Abigail told Mercy in 1775. "You will readily believe me when I say that I make no small sacrifice to the publick." "The frequent Absence of the best of friends," wrote Mercy to Abigail in 1776, "prevents to you and to me the full injoyment of the Many Blessing providence has kindly showered Down upon us. I sigh for peace yet it Cannot take place. But while the sword and the pestilence pervade the Land, and Misery is the portion of Millions, why should we

Expect to feel No interruption of Happiness." They understood each other as only two people in the same unhappy situation could.

Yet a significant power differential permeated the relationship. Mercy's interest in Abigail, while genuine, may also have had an ulterior motive. She may have cultivated Abigail in order to get greater access to John Adams. Despite her acceptance of traditional sex roles, Mercy felt somewhat constrained by those roles and was always sensitive to the limits placed on her by her gender. In her poem "On Primitive Simplicity," she had discussed "the narrow bounds, prescrib'd to female life." Though not acutely resentful of her position, she commented more than once that being a woman prevented her from actively venturing into the outside world. "I acknowledge we have an equal share of curiosity with the other sex," she explained to Abigail, ". . . [but men] have the opportunities of gratifying their inquisitive humour to the utmost, in the great school of the world, while we are confined to the narrow circle of domestic cares." Being "confined to the narrow circle of domestic cares" obviously did not fully satisfy Mercy's intelligence or temperament. First through her brother and father, then through her husband, she had gained some access to "the great school of the world."

Abigail's husband could provide Mercy with expanded horizons. In the early 1770s, John Adams was a rising young lawyer and an acknowledged political leader himself. As Mercy knew from his visits to her house, he was a man of learning and erudition, a man who was going places. John, however, had never expressed interest in Mercy, except insofar as she was his friend James's wife. Only after Mercy and Abigail had met in person, in 1773, did he begin to pay particular attention to Mercy. Only then did he request that she write a poem on the Boston Tea Party. Given this opening, Mercy seized the chance to initiate a separate correspondence with John.

Quickly completing John's assignment, she sent it off, in February 1774, in a letter addressed to Abigail, though she clearly was eager to hear John's opinion of her work. "I will not trust the partiality of My own sex so much as to rely on Mrs. Adams' judgment," she commented, "though I know her to be a Lady of taste and Discernment. If Mr. Adams thinks it deserving of any further Notice and he will point out the faults, which doubtless are many, they may perhaps be Corrected, when it shall be at his service." As much as she might have valued her friend's esteem, a man's opinion carried more weight. Fortunately for Mercy, John, as was mentioned, praised her effort lavishly. Claiming to be intimidated by his new friend, John quoted a line from Bishop Burnet to Lady Rachell Russell, a well-known British writer of the seventeenth century: "'Madam I never attempt to write to you but my Pen conscious of its Inferiority falls out of my Hand.'" A mutual admiration society was born.

Over the next several years, the two corresponded as often as John's busy schedule would admit. With the coming of war, his career flourished. Possessed of larger ambitions than James Warren, John moved from provincial politics to the national service, first by serving in Congress, then by becoming one of three Commissioners sent to France in 1778, then through other diplomatic missions in Holland and England. While it is unlikely that Mercy manipulated her friendship with Abigail only to get to John, the older woman clearly wanted to maintain a separate relationship with both parties. In subsequent letters to Abigail, she had no reservations about cajoling the wife to remind her husband to write to her. "I have sent forward My Letter to Mr. Adams," she reported to Abigail, "but Suppose I should have no answer unless Stimulated by you." She constantly pleaded for more letters from John himself. Women, she reminded him, "have some Curiosity as well as those who walk upon the surface of a World." Women's knowledge, she said, "is circumscribed within such Narrow Limits, and the sex [is] too often forbidden to taste the Golden Fruit." If John was Mercy's Adam, the forbidden fruit he offered her was political intelligence from the larger world.

Mercy's friendship with John Adams had great significance—emotional and symbolic—to her. In letters to John, Mercy flexed her intellectual muscles as she could with no other correspondent, with the important exception of the historian Catharine Macaulay. But John was male and held political power. He treated her as a confidant and an intellectual equal. He asked her advice on political matters and encouraged her to write about political issues. He enthusiastically supported her decision, made as early as 1775, to write a history of the American Revolution. She delighted in—and in a sense, depended on—his letters for affirmation of herself as an author and political being. "Your Criticism, or Countenance, your Approbation or censure," she told him, "may in some particulars serve to regulate my future Conduct." He became her mentor and, along with her husband, her most vocal supporter. Under his supervision her work flourished.

Even as Mercy's relationship with John expanded, her friendship with Abigail deepened. The two women comforted each other by letter and in person. Mercy sometimes stopped at the Adams's Braintree home on her way to or from visits with her husband, who was in Boston or Watertown on political business. Infrequently, Abigail would visit Mercy in Plymouth. Other ties bound the two families together. At the end of 1778, thirteen-year-old Nabby Adams came to stay with Mercy for a few months. With five sons and no daughters, Mercy had missed both the household assistance and female companionship that a daughter could have provided. Nabby supplied both. Mercy came to love her, and to "love her more the longer she resides with me." The families grew even closer.

From Abigail's perspective, Mercy continued to be a stimulating role model and a reliable confidant. She especially thought she had found a kindred spirit in locating another woman who was as preoccupied with politics as she. Yet Abigail had made a slight miscalculation. As political as she was, Mercy never shared Abigail's views on the rights of women. The differences became apparent in the aftermath of Abigail's now-famous letter to John to "Remember the Ladies." At this time, under the doctrine of coverture, women had no legal existence apart from the men in their lives. While they were single, women were under the guardianship of their fathers; after marriage, women were under their husbands' protection. They could not own property, could not sue or be sued, nor could they make contracts or wills. Widows were the only exceptions to these rules.

In 1776, while John was drafting the Massachusetts state constitution, Abigail made certain suggestions to him regarding the status of women. "And by the way," she wrote on March 31, "in the new Code of Laws which I suppose it will be necessary for you to make I desire you would Remember the Ladies, and be more generous and favourable to them than your ancestors. Do not put such unlimited power into the hands of the Husbands. Remember all Men could be tyrants if they could." In retrospect, it is unclear exactly what Abigail had in mind. Most historians now agree that she was not demanding that women be allowed to vote or hold public office. Perhaps emboldened by her own success in taking care of the Adams family farm, she was asking for expanded property rights or greater legal protection for women. She went on, however, to issue a warning, partly serious and partly jocular in nature. "If perticuliar care and attention is not paid to the Laidies we are determined to foment a Rebelion, and will not hold ourselves bound by any Laws in which we have no voice, or Representation."

Whatever she intended, John firmly rebuffed her. With a mixture of condescension and humor, he deflected her remarks. "As to your extraordinary Code of Laws, I cannot but laugh. . . . Depend upon it, We know better than to repeal our Masculine systems. Altho they are in full Force, you know they are little more than Theory. We dare not exert our Power in its Full Latitude. We are obliged to go fair, and softly, and in

Practice you know We are the subjects. We have only the Name
of Masters, and rather than give up this, which would
compleatly subject Us to the Despotism of the Peticoat, I hope
General Washington, and all our brave Heroes would fight."
Understandably, Abigail found John's reply less than satisfac-
tory.

Seeking a more sympathetic ear, she summarized the exchange for Mercy. "I thought it was very probable," she told
her friend, that "our wise Statesmen would erect a New
Goverment and form a new code of Laws. I ventured to speak
a word in behalf of our Sex, who are rather hardly dealt with
by the Laws of England which gives such unlimitted power to
the Husband to use his wife Ill." She mentioned her "threat"
that the women would stage a rebellion and John's infuriating
response. "He is very sausy to me in return for a List of Female
Grievances." Partly tongue-in-cheek, she suggested a joint
course of action. "I think I will get you to join me," she said,
"in a petition to Congress."

But Mercy was not interested in petitioning Congress for
women's rights. In fact, Mercy seems not to have replied to
Abigail's entreaty. Interpreting Mercy's silence, however, is
problematic. Other events at the time seem to have taken precedence over Mercy's correspondence. The Warrens' eldest
son, James, returned home from Harvard "disorderd in his
mind." Like his Uncle Jemmy, he apparently had suffered some
sort of emotional collapse. In her first letter subsequent to
Abigail's request, Mercy excused her silence, cryptically referring to a "want of Health, a Variety of Avocations, [and] some
A[n]xiety of Another Nature" that had prevented her from
writing sooner. Her son required more immediate attention
than her political musings.

Even without this distraction, however, Mercy may have been
less than receptive to Abigail's call for gender solidarity. Mercy
never called for the expansion of women's political or legal
rights. She mentioned the female franchise only once, in an

obsequious letter to Martha Washington soon after General Washington's election to the presidency. "I know not one [lady]," she told Martha, "who by general consent, would be more likely to obtain the suffrages of the sex . . . than the lady who now holds the first rank in the United States." In a more serious vein, Mercy had explained her understanding of the relationship of women to politics to Catharine Macaulay. "You see Madam," she wrote, "I disregard the opinion that women make but indifferent politicians. . . . When the observations are just and honorary to the heart and character, I think it very immaterial whether they flow from female lips in the soft whisper of private friendship or whether thundered in the Senate in the bolder language of the other sex." But as the full quote reveals, by the term "politicians" Mercy meant not elected officials, but political "theorists." As she saw it, women were qualified to think and write about politics, but she made an important distinction between the actions each gender was allowed to undertake.

Mercy accepted the prevailing notion that women exercised their greatest power over men through their private "influence." As she said in "The Squabble of the Sea Nymphs," "For females have their influence o'er kings/Nor wives, nor mistresses, were useless things." As wives and mothers, women could shape men's manners, morals, and political values. "The kind mother acts her little part/And stamps the tablet on the infant heart," she noted in "On Primitive Simplicity." No more direct political role was necessary. As a result, Mercy may not have responded to Abigail's appeal for support not simply because she was diverted by personal matters, but because she did not share the younger woman's views about the need for a "rebellion" by those of her sex. Though Mercy herself chafed at the constraints of the status quo, through her literary career she personally had found a way around them. Having made her own private accommodation, she did not envision a more general reform of sex roles. Mercy also may have had a more selfish reason for not supporting Abigail. Hearing of John's opposition to his wife's entreaties, Mercy may have believed that siding with Abigail might damage her cherished relationship with him. At this point, Mercy needed John too much to risk such a confrontation.

* * *

All the while, the war raged on. In an unexpected move, the British evacuated Boston on March 17, 1776. Viewing the ruins at Charlestown, Massachusetts, with Martha Washington, Mercy reported it to be "a Melancholy Sight, the last which Evinces the Barbarity of the Foe and leaves of deep impression of the Sufferings of that unhappy Town." In the years from 1775 to 1777, victories for the Americans were few and far between. The Continental Army failed in Canada, failed in New York City, and failed in Charleston, South Carolina. Triumphs at Trenton, Princeton, and Saratoga sustained the patriots' hopes, yet it was difficult to maintain the optimism of the prewar years. In 1778, Mercy summarized the situation for her husband: "Conspiracies at Cambridge, Traitors at Boston, . . . Burgoyne's troops supplied with arms, our own army without clothes, without provisions and without tents, many of them deserting to the enemy and others on the borders of mutiny. . . . Faith, fortitude and courage," she concluded, "are necessary to bear us up amidst the train of public evils."

In the ensuing years, American prospects for winning the war would improve, but the Warrens' own fortunes would decline. Although Mercy did not realize it at the time, the early to mid-1770s in many ways represented the peak of her life. An intoxicating cycle of debate, protest, and political activity had swept her into the vortex of the revolutionary movement. In certain circles, she was acknowledged to be the patriots' muse. Her political writings not only instructed and persuaded, they edified and stimulated the audience's literary sensibilities. She also found herself at the center of an extended epistolary network, corresponding with an illustrious group that included both prominent men and women. At the same time, her husband James occupied numerous positions of trust and responsibility within the Massachusetts government. He shouldered an enormous burden both before the war, by promoting the resistance against Britain, and during the conflict itself, when he helped build a new state government. The Warrens' extraordinary service allowed them to bask in the high esteem of their fellow patriots.

Soon, however, all that would change. The Revolution unleashed social and political changes the scope of which no one had anticipated. The Warrens would suffer in its wake. The optimism that had characterized their pre-revolutionary outlook, as well as their own reputations, went into decline—casualties of war.

CHAPTER FIVE

An Old Republican

The latter years of the war and the decade following the Revolution proved to be a time of immense turmoil for the Warrens. Their son's mental breakdown in 1776 had been the first blow—a subject so painful that Abigail Adams warned her husband not to ever mention it. In that same year, Mercy's health began to deteriorate. Always of a delicate constitution, she became increasingly subject to fainting spells, depression, and nervous headaches. By 1778, she frequently took to her bed to recover her strength and spirits. Soon, other, more tragic events involving her sons would make it even more difficult for her to maintain her equilibrium.

The family's political fortunes also suffered. Mercy's husband experienced a series of setbacks that led to his virtual withdrawal from politics. A new enemy emerged in the person of John Hancock, who began a concerted bid for power. Simultaneously, Mercy perceived the beginnings of a decline in public virtue, a drift away from the spirit of thriftiness, restraint, and self-sacrifice for the public good that had, in her eyes, made the Revolution possible. In its place, self-indulgence, luxury, and greed sapped the martial spirit and made republican government nearly impossible.

These tendencies and the widespread sense that the Union was on the verge of collapse, climaxed in Massachusetts with the major crisis of the Confederation—Shays's Rebellion. For Mercy, however, the solution seemed worse than the problem.

She, like other Antifederalists, saw the proposed Constitution of the United States as a betrayal of the Revolution. A self-styled "Old Republican," she regarded the proposed system as an insidious plot by designing men to subvert individual rights and replace it with a distant, aristocratic regime. She became a critic of the Constitution and a reluctant supporter of the new government. Alienation from politics and tragedy at home tinged Mercy's post-revolutionary experience with bitterness and grief.

* * *

After the evacuation of Boston in 1776, the main theater of war moved south, leaving the citizens of Massachusetts to turn their attention to internal affairs. They immediately focused on two main issues, the writing of a new state constitution and the implementation of measures to rein in a wildly inflationary currency, which was wreaking havoc on the economy. In the debate over these matters, two factions appeared. Samuel Adams and James Warren emerged as leaders of the "radical" party, a group that had supported the drive for independence from an early date but who now, having secured their goal, wanted to dampen popular sentiment for what they considered to be excessively democratic reforms. The so-called "moderates," led by John Hancock and other merchants, although once reluctant to sever ties with Britain, now adopted a politics that pandered—in their opponents' eyes—to popular wishes.

The changed political climate adversely affected James Warren's career. Early in the war, he had authored the controversial Act to Prevent Monopoly and Oppression, which fixed the prices of certain scarce goods. In late 1777, the legislature, sensing that the law was divisive and ineffective, openly repudiated Warren's strategy and repealed the statute. Shortly thereafter, the people of Massachusetts rejected the proposed state constitution that Mercy's husband had been instrumental in writing. In May 1778, his constituents handed him another defeat. They failed to reelect him, for the first time since

1766, to the Massachusetts House—a debacle Warren attributed to the malign influence of John Hancock and his followers. A further setback came the following autumn. With Hancock's support, the legislature passed a motion that permitted the return to Boston of certain well-to-do loyalists. To Warren and others, it seemed as if the Revolution was in danger of falling into the clutches of counter-revolutionaries who might undo all that they had done. "*Tempora Mutantur*," James lamented in a letter to John Adams.

The times were indeed changing. To chronicle the shift, Mercy authored a poem, published in the *Boston Gazette* of October 5, 1778, called, "The Genius of America weeping the absurd Follies of the Day." Picking up on James's lament, she began the poem, "O Tempora! O Mores!" "This piece was written," she observed in a note issued when the poem was republished in 1790, "when a most remarkable depravity of manners pervaded the cities of the United States, in consequence of a state of war; a relaxation of government; the sudden acquisition of fortune; a depreciating currency; and a new intercourse with foreign nations." Mercy sensed that a sea change had occurred in the nature of the revolutionary movement. In her husband's defeats she saw signs that virtue and reputation no longer commanded the respect they once had. In the demagoguery of Hancock and his ilk, she saw evidence that gross materialism and flagrant displays of wealth, especially by those who had not previously possessed it, held the day. Clearly alluding to the contrast between the virtue of the Adams-Warren faction and the depravity of the Hancock party, she decried the loss of public spiritedness she observed in political life:

> The selfish passions, and the mad'ning rage
> For pleasure's soft debilitating charms,
> Running full riot in cold avarice' arms;
> Who grasps the dregs of base oppressive gains,
> While luxury in high profusion reigns.
> Our country bleeds, and bleeds at every pore,

> Yet gold's the deity whom all adore;
> Except a few, whose probity of soul
> No bribe could purchase, nor no fears control.

As the war progressed, Mercy felt the ground shifting beneath her. Change in this context seemed to represent decline, a falling away from a high-water mark of virtue reached in the late 1760s and early 1770s. Yet there seemed to be nothing she could do to stop it.

Decline was a theme to which her pen would return many times in the late 1770s and 1780s. In her letters to John Adams, she reported that nothing short of a "Revolution in Manners" had occurred. "A state of war has ever been deemed unfavourable to virtue," she told Adams in 1778. "But such a total change of manners in so short a period, I believe was never known in the history of man. Rapacity and profusion, pride and servility, and almost every vice is contrasted in the same heart." The populace indulged in an orgy of consumption, buying newly available luxury items, hosting fancy balls, and conspicuously displaying their wealth. Wealth rather than virtue had become the test of merit for public figures. The result, she said, subverted "every principle of that republican spirit which requires patience, probity, industry, and self-denial." Even some of the leaders were not immune; many had "lost sight of their primeval principles, and the true interest of America."

New poems and plays, infused with the ethos of classical republicanism, expressed Mercy's continuing distress with the situation. In October 1779, she composed a poem called "Simplicity," which celebrated virtue as the hallmark of a self-governing people. Comparing the country to ancient Rome, she warned of the dangers of commerce, the loss of "simple manners," and of "soft, corrupt, refinements of the heart,/Wrought up to vice by each deceptive art." The results of such changes, she suggested, would be the nation's deterioration from a "golden age" to a state of "dark oblivion." A couple of years later, she reiterated the point in a play entitled *The Sack of Rome.* Set in ancient Rome and written in blank verse, the work depicted "the tumult and misery into which mankind are often plunged by an unwarrantable indulgence of the discordant passions of the human mind," as she put it in her introduction. Longer, with greater plot and fuller character development than her earlier plays, the work depicted the fate of the Emperor Valentinian and his family as the empire falls apart around them. Numerous betrayals, villainous murders, and unrequited loves kept the action moving. But the contemporaneous point was clear: "Empire decays when virtue's not the base,/And doom'd to perish when the parts corrupt." Another play written in the early 1780s, *The Ladies of Castile*, also portrayed the deleterious effects of declining virtue, this time in a Spanish context. Like her Puritan forbears, Mercy developed a penchant for jeremiads that predicted imminent gloom and doom if the people did not return to the paths of righteousness and morality.

Yet like the jeremiads, Mercy's declamations about the decline in public virtue cannot be taken at face value. As genuine as her concern was, she was steeped in an intellectual tradition derived from classical republicanism that stressed the inevitability of corruption, decay, and decline. Before the war, she had regarded Britain as the source of that corruption; now it seemed to emanate from within. While Mercy naturally wanted to combat what she saw as a disastrous alteration in the people's attitudes and behavior, she may have been battling a mirage. She had probably exaggerated the extent of Britain's prewar depravity and the prevalence of Americans' virtue. Now she had no one to blame for the country's problems but Americans themselves.

Just as important, Mercy found her own social position and her husband's political prominence challenged by the changes wrought by the Revolution. Both Warrens had grown up in a deferential society where the authority of their families was unquestioned. Their wealth and education assured them a place in the ruling class; they were society's natural leaders. When the time came, the men assumed they would be elected or appointed to positions of power. The women took it for granted that they would be viewed with the respect that derives from close association with those in power.

But the Revolution had produced unanticipated changes in American society. For one, it redistributed the wealth. Some individuals, especially farmers and merchants, made enormous profits selling goods to the Continental Army. Others, contrary to all high-minded principles, sold scarce goods to their fellow citizens at extortionate prices. The fluctuating currency also resulted in vast sums being made—and lost—producing, according to James Warren, "a great convulsion" in the economy. The paucity of hard money made it difficult for some people to buy the goods they wanted and needed. Many merchants went bankrupt, and the value of real estate depreciated. At the same time, certain currency speculators were able to make vast fortunes by playing on the uncertainties of the market.

As a result, the relations between the classes shifted. As they looked around them, the Warrens hardly recognized the new society that they had helped to create. James found the world turned "topsy turvy beyond the description of Hogarth's humorous pencil or Churchill's Satyr." His wife agreed. In her poem "The Genius of America," Mercy had written, "So dissolute—yet so polite the town/Like Hogarth's days, the world's turn'd upside down." Amplifying this theme, she told her son that the war "has nearly destroyed the proper ideas of subordination, decency, and civility among the lower classes." Old families that had dominated the region for generations lost wealth and prestige, only to be replaced by a nouveau riche, who did not show proper respect to their social betters. Perhaps even more annoying, the newcomers flaunted their money ostentatiously. "I am still drudging at the Navy Board for a morsel of Bread," James remarked to Adams in 1778, "while others, and among them fellows who would have cleaned my shoes five years ago, have amassed fortunes, and are riding in chariots." Mercy found such displays repugnant, even morally questionable. Though no aesthete, she cherished simple tastes. "Oeconomy," she once wrote to her granddaughter, "is a due mean between profusion and parsimony—the observation of that frugal elegance on the table, in dress and in furniture, which leaves sufficiency for the charities of life according to the degree of ability bestow[ed] by providence in the loan of its blessings." The Warrens and others of their social class felt their traditional authority slipping away—and they did not like it one bit.

These social shifts also altered the dynamics of political life. The old deferential rules governing the electoral process no longer pertained. The Revolution had politicized the population and given them a sense of their own power. The people of Massachusetts now expected their leaders to consult with them, and a new cohort of popular political leaders were willing to do just that.

The man who epitomized the worst of these changes, as the Warrens saw it, was John Hancock, the richest merchant in Boston. More than anything, Hancock aspired to political power, especially to the governorship of the state. As a member of Congress throughout the 1770s, he made frequent trips home to Massachusetts, where he made blatant attempts to win popular support. In December 1777, he donated 150 cords of wood to the town's poor. In February 1778, he placed an advertisement in the Boston papers noting that debts owed to him might be repaid in the plentiful paper currency rather than the scarce hard money. He purchased a concert hall for public use and on occasion supplied the audience with wine. He was also not above spreading malicious gossip about other public figures. People believed he was the source, for example, of a false rumor that Samuel Adams had been involved in a conspiracy to overthrow General Washington. Whatever Hancock's faults, he was successful and popular. Historian Gordon Wood notes that Hancock "formed one of the most elaborate networks of political dependency in eighteenth-century America."

To the Warrens, John Hancock was Thomas Hutchinson reincarnate. Hancock and his allies had, in fact, been Hutchinson supporters in the early 1770s, had opposed the nonimportation agreements, and had wavered on the question of independence. Hancock, Mercy commented in her *History of the American Revolution*, "though professedly in opposition to the court, had oscillated between the parties until neither of them at that time, had much confidence in his exertions." James was even more disgusted. "I cant bare the Influence," he wrote to Samuel Adams in 1778, "of Men who were so hid in Holes and Corners a few Years ago that it was difficult to find them; and when found dared not tell you which side they belonged to. . . . They most of them worship'd Hutchinson; they all now worship another who, if he has not H[utchinson]'s Abilities, certainly equals him in Ambition and Exceeds him in Vanity." The Warrens saw Hancock as the representative of superficiality, venality, and private ambition at the expense of the public good. In a letter written to John Adams in 1783, Mercy heaped venom upon her husband's rival. "A fortunate coincidence of circumstances has established [Hancock's] popularity," she wrote,

> and hung such a veil before the eyes of the vulgar, that nothing less than the convulsions of an Earthquake can rend it asunder; yet the reputation of this Idol of Straw has lately been in the wane; his obstinacy, vanity, levity, and ostentation have created disgust, and rendered him contemptible in the eyes of the soberer part of the community; but his partizans have influence enough to divide the Capital: to spread dissention among the people, and prejudices against the fairest patriots in the State.

To the Warrens' envy and dismay, Hancock had an instinctive grasp of the new realities of power that eluded the older leader. In this context, Mercy's complaints about the decline of civic virtue reflected less a diminution in public spirit and more her own unease with the changes undermining her family's power and position. If "party rage and luxury should cease," it would not, as she predicted in *The Sack of Rome,* necessarily lead to the restoration of empire. But it might recover the lost status of the Otises and the Warrens.

As much as they might try to blame Hancock, many of James Warren's political problems were of his own making. For a variety of complex reasons, Warren began to withdraw from public life in the mid-1770s. In March 1776, he submitted his resignation as paymaster general of the Continental Army to George Washington rather than accompany the army to New York. Later that year he was appointed Second Major General of the Massachusetts militia. But the following autumn he turned down the opportunity to lead his troops into battle. The next summer he resigned the post, claiming illness. In reality, he resented the fact that as a general in the militia he was subordinate in rank to all the officers of the Continental Army. In May 1776, he was offered an appointment to the Supreme Judicial Court of Massachusetts. Though a much sought-after position, James abruptly declined the honor. In October 1780, the General Court elected him to be the state's lieutenant governor; he refused to serve. In two different years the Massachusetts assembly chose him to be a delegate to the Confederation Congress; he failed to attend even one meeting. He did not, however, relinquish all of his public responsibilities. From 1776 to 1781 he served on the Navy Board and in 1779, 1780, 1781, and 1787 he represented his home constituency in the Massachusetts House of Representatives.

Warren seems to have made a deliberate decision to withdraw from government service. By 1778, he had served over twelve tumultuous years in the legislature, many of them away from home. The experience had exhausted him and made him yearn for peace. His farm and finances needed tending. He loved puttering around the Eel River estate, which had fallen into disarray during his absence. James, moreover, lacked the ambition for national office that drove men like John Adams to make continual sacrifices. Whereas Adams and others saw their destiny unfolding in national politics, Warren believed in a politics closer to home, grounded in local action and participation. "I am content," he told John Adams, "to move in a small sphere. I expect no distinction but that of an honest man who has exerted every nerve." Beyond that, the changed political climate left him bewildered and disgusted. "Wearied with the perplexities and embarrassments of public life, sickened by the ingratitude and baseness of mankind, and sighing for the felicity of domestic peace," James was ready, according to Mercy, "to leave the mazy paths of politics and war—and retire to the still, unvariegated scene of the sequestered roof."

Mercy herself may have been the precipitating factor in her husband's withdrawal from government service. As fascinating as she found politics, as important as it was to her to have access to the political realm, she had always hated her husband's absences on public business. "To J. Warren, Esq.," the poem she composed during her husband's first term in the legislature in 1766, bore the subtitle, "An Invitation to retirement." In it, Mercy contrasted the irritations of public service in "the noisy smoky town/Where vice and folly reign," with the Warrens' "peaceful calm retreat/Amidst the beautious plains." Even at that early date, she tried to lure him back home and out of politics. Mercy, it seems, found it nearly impossible to live without her husband. The couple's deep and enduring emotional intimacy depended on physical closeness. Each thrived in the other's presence and languished in the other's absence. As James's public service took him away from home more and more often, Mercy worried and waited. She was afraid that he would be assaulted by Hessians or Tories, terrified the he might suddenly be inspired to march off to battle, fearful that he would go away to attend meetings of Congress for months at a time. In a poem written for James in 1776, called "To Fidelio," Mercy mused on the joys of their relation-ship:

> 'Tis social converse, animates the soul.
> Thought interchang'd, the heavenly spark improves,
> And reason brightens by the heart it loves;
> While solitude sits brooding o'er her cares.
> She oft accelerates the ills she fears.

"All my Earthly Happiness," she once commented, "depend[s] on the continuance of his Life." James reciprocated her feel-ings. "When shall I hear from you[?]" he wrote in 1780. "My affection is strong. My anxieties are many about you. You are alone. You are very social. Your sensations are strong. . . . If you are not well and happy how can I be so [?]" On another occasion, he cut short a trip in order to return home early: "I need not tell you that I am Uneasy without you. . . . I feel so little satisfaction in my own mind and the days are so te-dious. . . . Everything appears so different without you." They literally could not bear to be apart for long periods.

Over time, Mercy needed James even more. Increasingly, she was sickly and bedridden, tormented by both physical and mental illnesses. After being inoculated for smallpox in 1776, her eyes began to bother her and her vision began to fail. To protect her eyes, she often had to sit in a darkened room. She frequently experienced "trembling Nerves" and long spells of low spirits. Like her brother and son, she may have suffered from a family predisposition toward depression. Only her hus-band could cheer her up, encourage her to pursue her liter-ary endeavors, and make her feel that life was worth living.

By the late 1770s, Mercy felt she could not sacrifice her husband for the country much longer. In "To Fidelio," she had made it clear that the country's gain was her loss:

> Yet while the state, by fierce internal war,
> Shook to the centre, asks his zealous care,
> I must submit, and smile in solitude,

My fond affection, my self love subdu'd":
The times demand exertions of the kind,
A patriot zeal must warm the female mind.

By 1780, her tolerance had reached its limit; she wanted her husband back. "I am sometimes Ready to think you could serve the public better unencumbered by anxieties for me," she told James in that year, but "I am not Hipocrite Enough to Conceal the secret Regrets that pray upon my mind & Interrupt my peace." Yet Mercy knew her decision was not blameless; she was no longer acting the part of a good Republican Wife. In 1778, after urging Abigail Adams to continue to allow John to serve in government, she defensively remarked, "Methinks . . . that you will justly say that we are very Ready to Give advice when we but Illy practice upon the principles we lay down. True," she admitted, "—but we may profit by the advice though we despise the Weakness of the Adviser." Whatever others might say, Mercy believed she and James had sacrificed enough for the cause. In their old age (they were by this time in their fifties), they thought they deserved to have the joy of one another's company.

Nonetheless, the question of public service was a sensitive one for leaders of the revolutionary generation. People such as George Washington, Thomas Jefferson, John Adams, and many lesser figures had little or no time to manage their farms or see their families. Their wealth declined; their personal lives suffered. But they endured it all for the sake of the patriotic cause. With so many people making superhuman sacrifices, those who did less than was expected of them were resented and shunned. On one occasion, Mercy had to apologize profusely to her friend Hannah Winthrop because her casual question about the absence of Hannah's husband from Congress had been construed as an insult. Mercy vehemently denied that "any question of mine with regard to Dr. Winthrop's absence from Congress looked like a suspicion that he was less attentive to the welfare of his country than usual." Those who could lead were expected to, whatever the toll it might take on their private lives.

Therefore, despite his many years of public service, James Warren's refusals to continue to serve gained him a reputation as a quitter, as someone whose willingness to sacrifice for the common good was in doubt. Many patriots never forgave him. John Adams frequently queried the Warrens on his friend's plans to return to the government. "It is too soon for Mr. Warren or me to retire," he wrote to Mercy in 1783. "Stability and Dignity must be given to the Laws, or our Labours have all been in vain and the old Hands must do this or it will not be done." Commenting on James's anticipated rejection of a judicial appointment, Abigail remarked to John, "I suppose it must be disagreable to him and his Lady, because he loves to be upon his Farm, and they both love to be together. But you must tell them of a Couple of their Friends who are as fond of living together, who are obliged to sacrifice their rural Amusements and domestic Happiness to the Requisitions of the public." To Adams and others, Warren's rejection of public responsibility was proof of a defect in character. "Warren has both Talents and Virtues beyond most Men in this World," Adams wrote to Abigail, "yet his Character has never been in Proportion. Thus it always is, has been, and will be."

Yet even without the burdens of public service, the post-Revolution years proved to be personally trying for the Warrens. In their passage to adulthood, their five sons experienced various traumas that inevitably affected the parents as well. The difficulties began in 1776 with the aforementioned mental breakdown of their eldest son, James. As she nurtured him toward recovery, Mercy surely wondered whether her son would follow in his Uncle Jemmy's footsteps and go completely mad. Upon recovering his spirits, the young James took the fateful step of enlisting in the American Navy. In 1781, while serving aboard the ship *Alliance* off the Maine coast, a British cannonball shattered his knee, necessitating the amputation of his lower leg. James returned home for a slow and painful convalescence. Other misfortunes followed. Mercy's third son, the mild-mannered Charles, soon contracted tuberculosis. Meanwhile, sensible, studious George had experienced great difficulties establishing himself in a career. Although he tried many things, including the law, he could never make a go of it. Eventually, he set out for the Maine frontier, where he farmed a tract of land owned by his father, built a house, and became a prominent local politician. Unfortunately, in 1800 George contracted a severe illness and died at the age of thirty-four, alone on his farm. Of all five Warren boys, only Mercy's fourth son, Henry, known for his vivacity and cheerfulness, lived a long, conventional, and relatively trouble-free life. He was also the only son to marry—a rather unusual fact considering the surplus of eligible women at the time in Massachusetts.

Yet it was her second son, Winslow, who caused Mercy the greatest joy and the greatest grief. Handsome, charming, and intelligent, Winslow was also inconsiderate, irresponsible, and immature. A risk taker and a bon vivant, he was as different from his dutiful, upright mother as someone coming from the same genes could have been. But Winslow was her favorite. He enchanted her, fired her imagination, opened up worlds that she hardly knew had existed. "You are possessed of a native greatness of soul which I have watched from your infancy," she wrote him, "and marked as capable of extremes of good or evil." Mercy took it as her task to act as his conscience and moral preceptor. "When I write to my son," she told him in 1784, "my pen as it were mechanically glides into a moralizing strain." Ultimately, however, she could not prevent his dark side from prevailing.

As he reached his late teens, Winslow refused to attend Harvard, the family alma mater. Instead, he made his way to Boston to establish himself as a merchant and entrepreneur. In the big city, he dabbled in foreign trade and tried to insinuate himself into the tight-knit merchant circles that had been so favorably disposed to his Uncle Jemmy. With the war on, however, trading was perilous and unprofitable. An inexperienced beginner found few opportunities. He did, however, have more success in the realm of pleasure, where he consorted with a variety of unsavory associates and showed a distinct fondness for gaming and the ladies.

One early incident reveals something of the dynamics between mother and son. During his stay in Boston, Winslow apparently became enamored of Lord Chesterfield's *Letters to his Son*. An advice book that counselled young men on the proper education, manners, and deportment of a gentleman, the work became the rage among the town's cosmopolitan elite. Published in 1774, with eighteen editions in twenty-five years, Chesterfield's letters eschewed traditional Christian ethics in favor of a social code based on hypocrisy and insincerity. According to Chesterfield, all social behavior was calculated to achieve certain ends, to create a public image. Morality, or inner virtue, was less important than the appearance of virtue. As a result, duplicity was not only tolerable, but inevitable, even desirable—especially, in his view, in one's romantic dealings with women.

While Chesterfield's theories appalled the proper Mercy, they appealed to the young Winslow, who like many others of his generation felt that the author spoke to him personally. To nip her son's enthusiasm in the bud, Mercy wrote Winslow a long letter critical of Chesterfield's ethics and reasoning. Despite occasional insights, she said, Chesterfield purveyed a kind of "honey'd poison . . . [that] sacrifices truth to convenience, probity to pleasure, virtue to the graces, generosity, gratitude, and all the finer feelings of the soul, to a momentary gratification." Knowing full well of her son's own susceptibility to such ideas, she insisted that he resist their appeal. "It is the race of fobs and fribbles, the half learn'd sceptic, the disciples of Hume and Bolingbroke, who are the devotees of a man, bold enough to avow himself the champion of every spieces of vice, only

cloathing it decently, that will subserve the guilty pleasure of
the accomplish'd debauchee." She was particularly outraged
by the author's attitude toward women: "I think his trite,
hackney'd vulgar observations, the contempt he affects to pour
on so fair a part of creation, are . . . beneath the resentment of
a woman of education and reflection. . . . I ever considered
human nature as the same in both sexes, nor perhaps is the
soul very differently modified by the vehicle in which it is
placed."

In late 1779 Mercy sent a copy of this letter to Abigail Adams,
who was so impressed that she forwarded it to the Boston *Independent Chronicle*, which immediately published it. Several other
publications also subsequently reprinted it. Unfortunately, the
letter had little effect on the person for whom it was intended.
Winslow continued to go his own way, regardless of his mother's
feelings. "I begin now to think Winslow does not Intend to
come & see me or that something Extraodinary has taken
place," Mercy wrote to her husband in March 1780. "Do tell
Winslow I am so often asked why he Never Comes that I am
tired of making excuses. I know I might be in a thousand situ-
ations more distressing than the present. Yet mine is very painful. I lie down in the Evening Grieved & Disappointed. Yet rise
in the morning with fresh hope, of Bliss." As much as he pained
her, Mercy continued to believe in Winslow.

Always the adventurer, Winslow imagined that his fortunes
would improve across the sea. Financed by his parents, he set
off for Holland in May 1780 at the age of twenty. Now apprehension about Winslow became a constant feature in Mercy's
daily life. She feared for his morality as well as his physical
safety. "You are going into a world of strangers," she told him,
"and at an early period of life entering alone a wide theatre of
action. . . . But you must remember in order to keep the mind
in due equilibrium that a youth blessed with many personal
accomplishments, warm in the pursuit of business, pleasure,
and the road to honour ought to be well acquainted with *him-*

self as well as with the history of *man.*" Warning him not to "barter" his soul "for the advantages reaped by the sycophant or the gambler, the votaries to beauty, or the sacrificers at the shrine of wealth without the chaplet of honour," she urged him to adhere to simple American virtues and values.

Subsequent events did not ease her mind. With the war still raging, Winslow's ship was seized by the British almost as soon as it reached the open seas, and he spent the summer as a British prisoner in St. John's, Newfoundland. Putting the best face on things, Mercy later wrote in her *History of the American Revolution* that her son had "voluntarily engaged to remain as an hostage till [an exchange of prisoners] might take place." In October, he was transported to London, where he made new acquaintances, including the artist John Trumbull of Connecticut, John Tyler of Boston, a gentleman of leisure, and an Englishman named John Temple. After numerous misadventures, including an interrogation by Lord Hillsborough and near capture as a suspected American spy, Winslow escaped to Holland in May 1781.

Always pursuing the unattainable, Winslow spent most of the next four years in Europe. John Adams reported seeing him once or twice in Amsterdam, but had little to report except that Winslow had "a general Reputation which he brought with him from Boston of loving Play"—hardly the words to ease an anxious mother's mind. At some point, the young rascal moved on to France, home of the philosophes—and of a whole new range of vices. Because of her staunch anti-Catholic, anti-aristocratic sentiments, Mercy feared that her son might be seduced by the polite, refined superficialities of a society that did not value hard work, frugality, and discipline. As she often did when overwhelmed by intense emotions, Mercy wrote a poem expressing her feelings. "To a Young Gentleman, residing in France," written in January 1782, warned Winslow of the evils of luxury, wealth, and aristocratic pretension. Mercy reiterated the value of "honest probity," and "economy" and warned her son to abandon his "illusive, airy chace,/And retrospect the happy path of peace." Urging him to come back to their loving home, she concluded saying, "Return, my son, for nothing else we need,/To see thee happy, would be bliss indeed." Once again, her plea fell on deaf ears.

Months passed in which the Warrens had no letter from him, no news of him. Typically, however, Mercy overlooked or forgave Winslow's faults. Though she sometimes disapproved of his actions, she could not disavow her favorite child. For one thing, she lived vicariously though him. While gender and temperament confined the mother to the "narrow circle of domestic cares," the son could explore "the great school of the world"—and report back his findings to her. Although she wanted him to remain upright and virtuous, she did not want her "maternal fears . . . to retard the manly pursuit[s]" in which he was engaged. Moreover, she never lost her belief in his natural talent. When he did write letters, they were masterly treatises, filled with fascinating details about his experiences, the habits of the people he met, the look of the countryside around him. He also charmed and flattered her. It was Winslow, Mercy said, "at whose Request a regular Dramatick Work was attempted." *The Ladies of Castile* was the result. Because of the special bond between them, no number of disappointments could ever completely disillusion her. She knew that with him, "I seem to be always tossing between Expectation & Disappointment." Though not blind to his shortcomings, she was an eternal believer in his infinite promise—and felt wounded afresh when he let her down, as he inevitably did.

By early 1783, Winslow apparently decided that he could not make a go of it in commercial trading abroad. The fledgling United States needed diplomats, he concluded, so he set his sights on obtaining a consular appointment. Arriving in May, he went straight to Philadelphia to make his case to Congress. Habitually insensitive to his parents' feelings, he shamelessly sought their assistance in his new endeavor. Obliging parent that he was, James tried to help him, but he failed. "My days of influence are over," he concluded unhappily. After some tense moments in which Mercy heard rumors to the effect that her son would return to Europe without seeing her, Winslow deigned to visit for eight months.

But the larger world continually beckoned. In April 1784, Winslow set sail for Portugal, armed only with the vague hope that a consular appointment would soon materialize. Shortly thereafter, his brother Charles's case of tuberculosis took a turn for the worse. Grasping at straws, in the autumn of 1785 the Warrens put Charles on a ship headed for Lisbon, where, they hoped, the temperate climate and Winslow's company would improve their son's health. Unbeknownst to them, however, Winslow, in debt and disappointed that the desired sinecure had not materialized, had already departed the continent. On December 8, Winslow arrived, unannounced, at the Warren household in Milton. Though thrilled to see him, Mercy and James were horrified at the thought of Charles arriving in Lisbon, sick and alone. In yet another painful irony, however, they soon learned that Charles had, at the tender age of twenty-three, died en route to Europe, having resisted the deathbed attempts of a Catholic priest to convert him to papistry. Mercy had regained one son only to lose another.

* * *

As insistent as the Warrens' personal problems were at this time, their crises paled in comparison with those faced by the nation as a whole. After the Revolutionary War ended in 1783, the nation faced a crisis of confidence and identity. It was one thing for thirteen fractious, heterogeneous states to unite in a defensive union to fight against Britain; it was quite another for them to compromise and cooperate without the pressure of an imminent threat. Abroad, many foreign nations failed to receive American ambassadors or did not accord them the proper respect. At home, Congress could barely manage its own affairs. Money was a constant problem. Because it lacked the power to tax directly, Congress could only request voluntary sums from the states, which they often refused to pay in whole or in part.

Moreover, many state legislatures passed laws that contravened the federal government's authority. For example, some states failed to compensate loyalists for confiscated property—in direct violation of the U.S. treaty ending the war with Great Britain. Other states injured the long-term economic interests of citizens by erecting tariff barriers or printing enormous sums of paper money. If the colonies had come to maturity with independence, they were now, in Mercy's eyes, once again reduced to "a state of infancy. As a child just learning to walk, they were afraid of their own movements. Their debts were unpaid, their governments unsettled, and the people out of breath by their long struggle for the freedom and independence of their country." To prevent the Union from falling apart, significant changes in the structure of the federal government seemed necessary.

As its leaders were pondering what to do, an event occurred that pushed the country into action. During the fall of 1786, political discontent in western Massachusetts erupted into violence in what became known as Shays's Rebellion. Westerners within the state felt especially put upon by the consequences of a postwar economic depression. At the same time, legislators in Boston passed a series of heavy taxes, to be paid in hard currency, in order to pay off the state's war debt. Underrepresented and overly burdened by the taxes, the westerners initiated a series of protests to express their dissatisfaction with the government.

The westerners saw their protests as following in the same pattern laid down by the revolutionaries just a decade earlier. Like the patriots, they opposed unjust taxation policies levied by a distant and unresponsive legislature. Like the revolutionaries, they voiced their objections through peaceful protests, including petitions, instructions to the assembly, and the calling of county conventions. But the Massachusetts assembly, dominated by eastern merchants, many of whom were creditors, refused to address the westerners' grievances or grant them economic relief. By the autumn of 1786, the situation had reached a crisis. The state used the courts to confiscate the land of those farmers who could not pay their taxes, thereby depriving them of their livelihood and, of course, their only means of repaying their debts. As the westerners saw it, the government had become as tyrannical as Britain was before the Revolution. Under the nominal leadership of Daniel Shays, a former captain in the Continental Army, they took up arms to protect their property and defend their rights. They drilled in militia musters and closed the county courthouses, thus preventing any further foreclosures. Though the number of violent incidents was small, the fact that the Shaysites were willing to press their claims through force of arms caused widespread alarm among the nation's political elite.

Throughout the states, political leaders construed Shays's Rebellion as symptomatic of a general decline into anarchy and violence, the first stage in the breakup of the Union. They believed that swift action was necessary to quash the movement. Although Massachusetts Governor James Bowdoin appealed to the Confederation Congress for help, under the terms of the Articles of Confederation, the federal government had no direct power to call up troops. Disgusted by Congress's weakness, Bowdoin turned to neighboring states, who sent in their state militias. By early 1787, the insurrection had been crushed. Yet Shays's Rebellion became a symbol for all that was wrong with government under the Articles of Confederation and a catalyst for the calling of the federal constitutional convention.

Like many other Americans, Mercy categorically rejected the comparison between the Shaysites and the revolutionaries. While she believed that rebellion could sometimes be justified against a tyrannical monarch, it was never legitimate against a constitutional government of the people's own making. As she observed in her *History of the American Revolution*,

The ignorance of this incendiary and turbulent set of people might lead them to a justification of their own measures, from a recurrence to transactions in some degree similar in the early opposition to British government. . . . They knew that a successful opposition had been made to the authority of Britain, while they were under the dominion of the king of England; but they were too ignorant to distinguish between an opposition to regal despotism, and a resistance to a government recently established by themselves. . . . They were violating the constitutions of their own forming, and endeavouring to prostrate all legal institutions, before they were cemented on the strong basis of a firm and well established government.

Her family backed up her words with action. The Warrens' son, Henry, and their nephew, Harrison Gray Otis, served with the troops sent in to put down the revolt.

For James Warren, the uprising provided an opportunity to reenter state politics. Having sat out of the legislature since 1781 and been defeated for governor in 1785, he put himself forward as a candidate for the lower house in 1787. In a wave of general revulsion against the government's treatment of the Shaysites, the people of his town chose him to serve. Back in the legislature, members promptly elected him to his old post as Speaker of the House.

But his position of prominence got him into trouble. Although he had not supported the Shaysites' aims or methods, he did sympathize with their plight as debtors. He believed that the legislature had not addressed the Shaysites' legitimate complaints and had taxed them unfairly. Moreover, he denounced as repressive certain measures taken by the General Court to put down the rebellion, which had included suspending the writ of habeas corpus, depriving former Shaysites of their civil liberties, and providing for the trial of rebels outside the counties of their residence. For his candor, James suffered. From this point on, he, too, was branded a Shaysite and faced constant vilification for his alleged support of the rebellion. In 1788, he lost the race for lieutenant governor partly because of his purportedly radical associations.

In the wake of Shays's Rebellion, delegates gathered in Philadelphia in May 1787 to discuss proposals for revising the Articles of Confederation. Most thinking Americans agreed that the Articles were fatally flawed; a stronger central government was necessary to insure the preservation of the Union. Even Mercy agreed: "Since her dismemberment from the British empire, America has, in many instances, resembled the conduct of a restless, vigorous youth, prematurely emancipated from the authority of a parent, but without the experience necessary to direct him to act with dignity or discretion." But the dimensions of the needed change were unclear. People wondered how drastically the Articles should be revised. Could the federal government be strengthened without infringing on the people's rights and liberties? As Mercy put it to Catharine Macaulay, "Our situation is truly delicate and critical. On the one hand, we stand in need of a strong federal government, founded on principles that will support the prosperity and union of the colonies. On the other we have struggled for *liberty* and made costly sacrifices at her shrine and there are still many among us who revere her name too much to relinquish beyond a certain medium, the rights of man for the dignity of government." The first action of the delegates, to close the proceedings to the public, did not inspire confidence in people like Mercy. "It was thought by some," she noted, ". . . that the greatest happiness of the greatest number was not the principal object of their contemplations, when they ordered their doors to be locked, their members inhibited from all communications abroad, and when proposals were made that their journals should be burnt, lest their consultations and debates be viewed by the scrutinizing eye of a free people. . . . It is certain, that truth, whether moral, philosophical, or political, shrinks not from the eye of investigation."

The product of the debates—an entirely new form of government as evinced in the proposed federal Constitution—

pleased Mercy even less. The new system would strengthen the powers of the central government by giving it the right to tax, regulate interstate commerce, and call up federal troops. But the proposal still allocated certain powers to the states; it was, according to *Federalist* # 39,[1] "neither wholly national nor wholly federal." The new system also gave the people a direct say in the national government. "Successive filtrations," as James Madison called them, would preserve the people's voice and at the same time, modify it through the election of judicious rulers who would legislate in the best interests of the entire country. Power would be divided among the executive, legislative, and judiciary branches, with numerous checks on each by the other.

The delegates to the Constitutional Convention believed that they had created "a machine that would go of itself," a form of government that would guarantee the people's liberties even if the people themselves were not virtuous. The Constitution took what was best from history and blended it with the hard lessons Americans had learned by governing themselves since independence. While the Convention had exceeded its charge by proposing a whole new form of government rather than by revising the old system, it had stipulated that the Constitution could go into effect only when nine of the thirteen states had approved it by means of specially elected ratifying conventions. The people would have to give their explicit approval to a new system.

For Mercy and her husband, the proposed Constitution was as a red flag to a bull. While acknowledging the need for reform, the Warrens regarded the proposed scheme as a dangerous innovation, which strengthened the national govern-

---

[1]The Federalist papers consisted of a series of eighty-five essays written by James Madison, Alexander Hamilton, and John Jay to promote ratification of the Constitution in New York. Highly influential at the time, they were reprinted in newspapers throughout the country. Since then, they have become the foremost source for understanding the framers' interpretation of the Constitution.

ment at the people's expense. Like other Antifederalists, they criticized the document on several grounds. The Constitution, they said, attempted to impose a single republican form of government over a country that was far too large, heterogeneous, and conflictual to contain it. The new Congress would take away power from the state legislatures and erode popular control over the democratic process. The national government would be too distant, too aristocratic, and too removed to serve the people's needs. And most important, the Constitution contained no bill of rights; there were no explicit guarantees of the protection of individual civil liberties. As they saw it, acceptance of the new government would signal a return to some of the worst aspects of British rule.

As Antifederalists, the Warrens joined a cohort of political leaders who had supported the Revolution but who now rejected the proposed Constitution. Known variously as "Old Republicans," "Old Patriots," or "Old Revolutionaries," the group included Samuel Adams, Patrick Henry, George Mason, Richard Henry Lee, and Charles Carroll. What these individuals had in common, according to historian Pauline Maier, was their age and formative political experiences. Leading supporters of the Constitution tended to be younger, having come of age by serving in national political institutions such as the Continental Congress or Army; their politics, according to Maier, "were formed within institutions born of the Revolution." But the leading Antifederalists were older, having been born during the 1720s and 1730s. Their crucial political experiences had occurred in provincial rather than national institutions, and their primary loyalty remained with their respective states rather than with the nation. James Warren, born in 1726, who rose to prominence in the Massachusetts assembly in the 1760s, fit the Antifederalist generational mold precisely; Mercy, who gained her political experience vicariously, also reflected this model.

Both James and Mercy aired their opposition to the Constitution in public forums, though like other Antifederalists, they cloaked their true identities by using pseudonyms. Writing as "A Republican Federalist," James published a series of seven articles in the *Massachusetts Centinel* in late 1787 and early 1788. In closely reasoned fashion, he constructed a narrow argument scrutinizing the Constitution on its technical shortcomings and inadequacies. He faulted the plan for its proposed system of representation. He criticized the document for bypassing the state legislatures and allowing conventions of the people in each state to ratify the Constitution. Most important, he challenged the plan's very legitimacy. By proposing a whole new form of government rather than revising the Articles, the framers, he said, not only exceeded the mandate given them by the states, but threatened the stability of the Union. "Of all compacts," he said, "a Constitution or frame of Government, is the most solemn and important, and should be strictly adhered to. The object of it is the preservation of that property, which every individual of the community has, in his *life, liberty* and *estate*. Every measure therefore, that only approaches to an infraction of such a covenant, ought to be avoided, because it will injure that sacred regard to the Constitution which should be deeply impressed on the minds of the whole community." James saw the Constitution for what it was: a bloodless coup d' état, and he claimed that such a move was neither necessary nor desirable.

Mercy took a different approach. In February 1788, she published a pamphlet in Boston under the pseudonym "A Columbian Patriot." Written in her typically bombastic, convoluted style, the work nonetheless represented a tour de force against the proposed system of government. Once again demonstrating her acute political sense, the author raised many of the standard Antifederalist concerns against the Constitution, including its lack of a bill of rights, the difficulty, if not impossibility, of preserving republican government in such an extensive territory, the threat posed by a standing federal army, and the inadequacy of the proposed representation in Congress. But she went beyond the usual Antifederalist criticisms.

Whereas the framers believed their eclectic combination of checks and balances would guarantee individual liberty, Mercy found a disaster in the making. To her, the proposed scheme was a "many-headed monster; of such motley mixture, that its enemies cannot trace a feature of Democratick or Republican extract; nor have its friends the courage to denominate it a Monarchy, an Aristocracy, or an Oligarchy, and the favoured bantling must have passed through the short period of its existence without a name, had not Mr. *Wilson* . . . suggested the happy epithet of a *Federal Republic*." Whereas Federalists portrayed their handiwork as the best plan human minds could devise, Mercy found it lacking; there was too much room for human error, corruption, and greed. "Let the best informed historian produce an instance," she challenged, "when bodies of men were intrusted with power, and the proper checks relinquished, if thy were ever found destitute of ingenuity sufficient to furnish pretences to abuse it." The Constitution represented a dangerous experiment that threatened to undermine the very liberties fought for in the American Revolution. "The glorious fabric of liberty successfully reared with so much labour and assiduity totters to the foundation," Mercy declaimed, "and may be blown away as the bubble of fancy by the rude breath of military combinations, and politicians of yesterday." She begged the states that had not yet voted to reject the document or postpone their proceedings indefinitely.

Despite their common opposition to the Constitution, Mercy and James's essays highlighted the contrast between their minds as well as their prose styles. Whereas James made small careful points, whittling away at the Constitution's technical validity, Mercy made grand sweeping arguments that attacked the assumptions behind the entire document. While he tried to chip away at it using closely reasoned legalities, she employed sweeping allusions to ancient Roman history and French Enlightenment philosophy to highlight its inadequacies. Whereas he was sober and restrained, she was ambitious and dramatic, even histrionic. It was Mercy's pamphlet, however, that appears to have been the more influential. While his was published only in Boston, hers was printed in several newspapers in New York and reprinted in other states. It has subsequently become an Antifederalist classic. With justifiable pride, she sent a copy to Catharine Macaulay in December 1787. Without ever explicitly challenging the gender boundaries that limited her career, Mercy managed to function extremely effectively within those constraints—at times performing better than her husband.

Perhaps because of his views, James had failed to win election to the Massachusetts ratifying convention. Despite the Warrens' best efforts, the state, with much dissension, did approve the Constitution. By July 1788, a two-thirds majority of the states had assented to the document, insuring its acceptance. Like other Antifederalists, once the new government was formally approved, the Warrens abandoned their public opposition. Privately, however, Mercy did not give the new government much of a chance for success. "We are too poor for Monarchy—too wise for Despotism, and too dissipated, selfish, and extravagant for Republicanism," she moaned to Macaulay. Supporters of the Constitution nevertheless acted quickly to quell their opponents' doubts. Once the new government went into operation, Congress passed a list of amendments that would safeguard individual rights and liberties, which they then sent to the states for approval. Known as the Bill of Rights, these amendments helped convince skeptics that a strong centralized government was not incompatible with a respect for civil liberties. "When the amendments took place immediately on its adoption," Mercy admitted in her *History of the American Revolution*, "the government of the United States stood on a basis which rendered the people respectable abroad and safe at home." The Bill of Rights helped reconcile the Warrens to the new order of things.

They reconciled themselves so quickly, in fact, that Mercy soon began to appeal to their highly placed friends in the new administration to obtain sinecures for her sons. Their old friend John Adams was now vice president; another acquaintance, Henry Knox, was secretary of war; others, including Elbridge Gerry, sat in Congress. Mercy felt no reticence or embarrassment about approaching her friends for political favors. She maintained that patronage was a legitimate perquisite of power. The Otis family had long used their connections to provide positions for one another: her father had done it for her brother; her brother had done it for her husband and his father; now she would do it for her sons. As she saw it, such positions represented a repayment for the family's exertions and sufferings during the Revolutionary War. She was not asking for "a stipend, or a liberal donation." Rather, she told Elbridge Gerry, sinecures represented "[the] property advanced for the public weal . . . for the payment of which the public Honor and equity was pledged, and which every honest man in Government must blush to see withheld from a faithful servant of the United States." Mercy asked Secretary Knox to appoint her son Henry as collector of customs for Plymouth or Duxborough. He turned her down. Undeterred, she petitioned for another position, this time for the troubled Winslow.

Since returning from Europe, Winslow had continued his slide into iniquity. He still dabbled in trade, with no greater success than before. Eventually, his luck ran out. In March 1786, he was served with a writ for appearance for debts that he owed to one John Codman, a merchant. Angrily, Winslow sought out his antagonist and, in a scene eerily reminiscent of his uncle's beating by John Robinson, caned Codman on the floor of the Boston Stock Exchange. Sent to jail in New Haven in November, Winslow quickly escaped. Desperate to rein him in, his parents shipped him off to Maine to help his brother George farm the family lands. But Winslow missed the excitement and sociability of the city, and he soon resurfaced in Boston.

Hoping to turn him around, Mercy attempted to secure for Winslow a military appointment in the new U.S. Army. Writing to Knox in 1791, Mercy described herself as "a mother who suffers too much from the injurious and unjust persecution of nefarious men towards a son possessed of generosity, dignity, and a thousand other amiable qualities, though he has been *unfortunate.*" Unmoved, Knox politely referred her request to President Washington. Mercy thought her best chance, however, lay with John Adams, who had recently returned from Europe and now, of course, occupied the second-highest position in the government. Invoking their years of friendship, she asked him to use his influence to obtain a commission for Winslow. "[You] have reached the acme of applause," she wrote him, "and are placed in a situation to do eminent service to your country, to establish your family and to assist most *essentially* your friends."

But the years had tattered the friendship between the Warrens and the Adamses. After the war ended, their paths diverged. John pursued a high-powered political career as a diplomat in France and England. Eventually, Abigail joined him abroad, getting a chance to experience for herself "the great school of the world"—something her friend Mercy, who had never ventured outside of Massachusetts, had never done. Over time, John's conceptions of government had changed. Many people regarded his *Defense of the Constitution of the Government of the United States*, written in 1787–1788, as a brief in defense of monarchy and a repudiation of the "old republican" principles for which they had fought the Revolution. For their part, the Adamses had grown increasingly suspicious of the Warrens' loyalty and patriotism. They resented James's early retirement from government service, and they erroneously believed the Warrens to have supported Shays's Rebellion. They correctly understood the family to have opposed the Constitution—and disdained them for it. Mutual distrust and wariness had replaced the former spirit of goodwill and common support for a shared enterprise.

Under these circumstances, Mercy's blunt and unsophisticated request for assistance offended the new vice president, and he did not hesitant to tell her so. "In the first place," he told her, "I have no patronage; in the next, neither your children nor my own would be sure of it if I had it. Beyond my own clear conviction of the public good I should belie the whole course of my public and private conduct and all the maxims of my life, if I should ever consider public authority entrusted to me to be made subservient to my private views, or those of my Family or Friends." In truth, John seemed to have no problem extending patronage to his nephews and other favorites. But he was not about to use his influence for the tarnished Warrens. Unfortunately, the incident alienated the families permanently; after that, their friendship never really recovered its old warmth.

Failing to take the hint, Mercy went to an even higher authority for help—to Washington himself. In a craven attempt to curry favor, she dedicated her first book, a collection called *Poems, Dramatic and Miscellaneous,* to the president. She called Washington a man "who has united all hearts in the field of conquest, in the lap of peace, and at the head of government." In just a few short years, she would come to scorn Washington as a man "much depreciated in my esteem," diminished as a result of "his avarice of that base incense of adulation which he snuffs with avidity from every pen and every tongue of a servile generation." At the time of her request, however, she herself was not above such "adulation."

In the meantime, Winslow could not keep himself out of trouble. Completely bankrupt, he now faced lawsuits from various creditors. The federal Circuit Court in Boston, in one of its first decisions, ruled against him and sent him to jail for a month. Denied all privileges, even that of exercising in the prison yard, he appeared to have no more options. As defensive of her son as ever, Mercy excoriated the agents of his punishment. "I think there is no reason," she wrote to Winslow, "to palliate the conduct of the Circuit Court; a corrupt influence is apparent; and added to the high handed designs of *Federalism,*—the vindictive spirit of Codman and Lowel [the merchants to whom Winslow owed money] have procured a decision disgraceful to humanity." Finally, however, Mercy's entreaties to those in high places appeared to have some effect. In May 1791, Winslow was appointed a Second Lieutenant in the Second Regiment of the U.S. Army. By the next month, he received orders to march under the leadership of General Arthur St. Clair to the western frontier. He left without even having time to say good-bye to his mother.

Mercy, of course, was frantic. Though recent events had finally dampened somewhat her enthusiasm for her favorite son (she was "pained at the new stile of life" he had adopted), she still believed in him. She urged him to carry both a Bible and a pen with him westward. She hoped he would write, for he would find a whole new realm of experience on the frontier. Your "genius," she said, "will lead you to a thousand observations worth preserving." But this was not to be. Unfortunately, St. Clair happened to be one of the most inept and misguided of the young country's generals. After a long journey, his troops set up camp in the Ohio wilderness, near the banks of the Miami River. Early on the morning of November 4, 1791, a band of local Indians, armed by the British, snuck up on the unsuspecting soldiers as they slept. The result was a massacre. Of the 1,400 men under St. Clair, nearly half were killed or reported missing. Among the dead was Second Lieutenant Winslow Warren.

Mercy was inconsolable. Her worst fears had been realized. For months afterward she could not write; she could not think; she could not sleep. She could only weep and mourn her lost son. By the following February, she continued to chastise herself. "Oh how I do regret that we did not all write to prevent if possible our dear Winslow engaging in the late fatal expedition," she told her son George. "For myself, I have never had a moment's quiet, since I saw the direction that announced his appointment. Yet I dared not disclose the feelings of my soul, for fear of imputation of *womanish weakness*, maternal anxiety, and the creation of apprehensions and dangers that had only an imaginary existence." Though her grief became less intense over time, it never disappeared completely. She publicly attacked Washington's Indian policy and became an implacable enemy of the Federalist party.

Eventually, as she had done after her other sons' deaths, she wrote an elegy for Winslow. In each of the prior memorials, she had stressed the hope of eternal life and the necessity of resignation to the will of God. The poem for Winslow did not display a stoic acceptance of death. "Written in deep affliction," as she called it, reflected Mercy's desperate effort to contain her grief. It was the most heartfelt, and also the most beautiful, of the poems to her sons. She lovingly recalled his person—a brow that was "fair as Eastern morn,/His mind with wisdom's maxims fraught." Recounting the circumstances of his death, she shuddered to think of him "Entomb'd beneath a distant oak." Time had not yet dulled her pain. Her grief, she said, "was too great to be express'd"; her heart was still "*bleeding.*" In a passage evocative of the sentiments of a later female poet, Emily Dickinson,[2] Mercy described the state of her soul

> Each fibre's chill'd—the frozen tears
> Refuse their wonted aid to lend
> In woes 'lorn garb I silent mourn
> My filial son—my faithful *friend.*

Although she concluded with a bow to conventional forms, hoping to meet her son once again "Amidst a bright Angelic choir," the prospect of a future heavenly encounter did not seem to diminish her present sorrow.

---

[2]There is a similarity to Dickinson's poem, "After great pain, a formal feeling comes." The most relevant stanza reads: This is the Hour of lead–/Remembered, if outlived,/As freezing persons recollect the Snow–/First–Chill–then Stupor–then letting go.

There is no evidence that Dickinson knew Warren's work.

As painful as Mercy found Winslow's death, her relationship with her favorite son revealed in acute form one of her most serious personality flaws: she constantly blamed others for her family's failures. She always felt that her family members were being unfairly attacked or persecuted. When her father or brother suffered a setback, Thomas Hutchinson and his evil allies had sponsored it. When her husband failed in some political maneuver or election bid, John Hancock or the "vindictive spirit . . . of party malice" was to blame. When her sons got in trouble, "the injurious and unjust persecution of nefarious men" had to be behind it. She personalized politics to such an extent that her relatives' failure inevitably represented the failure of the entire political system as well. Rather than see misfortune as the result of individual error, personal inadequacy, or just bad luck, she projected responsibility for her relatives' mistakes onto other individuals or groups.

And for Winslow—who never treated his mother with the respect she deserved, who conned, lied, and cheated his way through life—she had the most excuses of all. "No one knew better than myself the assemblage of great and good qualities that adorned the unfortunate, filial son," she told her son James, after Winslow's death. "But fortune forbad the full display of his talents, while it brightened his equanimity and his fortitude through the most extraordinary series of disappointments and persecution from men far, very far beneath him, in every thing but the possession of a little more gold." So blinded was she by love and loyalty that she could never admit that her relatives made mistakes, or worse, did bad things. Seen as eternal victims, they also were not in control of their own fates. Mercy's saving grace, however, was that she did not extend to herself the same dispensation that she gave to the others. She knew that *she* made mistakes—the consequences of which she was quick to accept. "Our happiness," she once told her son Henry, "depends on ourselves, on the calm and equal state of our own minds and not on the versatile conduct of others."

Unfortunately for Winslow, Mercy's continual willingness to find excuses for him meant that he never took full responsibility for his actions—until, finally, he paid the ultimate price for his choices.

* * *

Winslow's death capped more than a decade of political disappointments and personal tragedies for the Warrens: the mental breakdown and physical crippling of their eldest son, James; Charles's death at sea; unfair association with Shays's Rebellion; the ratification of a Constitution they opposed; James Senior's electoral defeats, and a painful investigation into his conduct at the Navy Board (in which he was eventually exonerated). And yet, the 1780s had begun auspiciously enough. In one of the great ironical acts of their time, Mercy and James Warren purchased Thomas Hutchinson's country house at Milton Hill in 1781. Located only fourteen miles from Boston, the fine one and one-half story house perched atop a hill overlooking the Neposet River, with a view north to Boston Bay. Fabled for its sylvan setting, it was subsequently called a "Monticello in Massachusetts." Because of its proximity to the capital, Mercy no longer had to endure the prospect of extended separations from her husband. Moreover, the Warrens now had an elegant residence in which to receive guests. Throughout the decade, Mercy and her husband entertained many illustrious visitors, including the Marquis de Lafayette, Francisco de Miranda, and Catharine Macaulay, whom Mercy finally met face-to-face after corresponding with her for over a decade.

Mercy and James loved their new home. "Nature has ornamented this place with a liberal hand," she wrote to Winslow in 1784. "It possesses many advantages both for business and pleasure." But the purchase of "Tremont," as she called it, proved to be a grave misstep. The couple had paid "a great sum" for the estate, forcing them into debt at a time when fluctuations in the currency made indebtedness highly risky. As it turned out, they could not afford the indulgence. Although James found it, he said, "Too sweet a place to part with," he received no help from his sons in farming the land or otherwise making it profitable. In the end, it was too much for them. In 1788, they sold the house and returned to Plymouth, exhausted and forlorn by the events of a turbulent decade. This dream, too, had soured on them.

CHAPTER SIX

"History is not the Province of the Ladies"

Toward the end of her life, Mercy summarized her generation's collective experiences to John Dickinson. "We have lived," she said, "in a period of more sudden revolution, more rapid and unexpected danger, interesting to the state of society and of Nations, than have perhaps been witnessed by any of the gazing Spectators on the events of time, within the short limits of thirty years." The last quarter century of her life, from 1789 to 1814, proved to be no exception. During that period, Mercy witnessed the implementation of the U.S. Constitution, the outbreak of the French Revolution, the emergence of political factions in Congress, the threat of armed conflict with France, and the entry of the United States into another war with Great Britain. Unlike the events of her earlier life, however, she and her husband now observed these phenomena from a distance; they lived largely outside the political orbit. While she continued to take an interest in the affairs of state, she felt alienated from the sources of power and skeptical about the nation's future.

In her last quarter century, however, Mercy's most important project was, in a sense, herself. At the age of sixty-two, she published her first book, consisting of a collection of her poems and plays. In 1805, she issued her most enduring accomplishment, the *History of the American Revolution*, a work that had taken over thirty years to complete. In these writings, Mercy articulated a new understanding of herself as a woman author. Although she never overtly rejected the patriarchal structure of society, she became more assertive about her right to express herself on political matters. Shedding her earlier timidity, she argued that women contributed an important and distinctive voice in political affairs.

This newfound sense of self proved to be essential in defending her work from criticism, especially that of her former mentor, John Adams. Upon reading her *History*, Adams attempted to discredit her sources and disavow her study. He bitterly denounced Mercy as a historian, a writer, and a woman. Despite the pain of this rejection, Mercy responded to his attacks with dignity and good sense. Even Adams's tirades could not shake her fundamental sense of self-righteousness. It was perhaps the final irony of Mercy's life that the person who had been so instrumental in furthering her career ended up repudiating her masterwork.

* * *

The political battles of the 1780s had alienated Mercy from the political process. As early as 1786, she told Samuel Adams that her husband and family "seem[ed] to be forgotten" and that she was now assuming the role of "silent spectator." In 1792, though a "kind of revolution in politics" sent her husband back into government as a member of the Governor's Council for a few years, Mercy remained aloof from the day-to-day issues of governing. When her son George ran for a seat in the Massachusetts legislature from his home district in Maine, she pointedly observed, "You seem to have an hereditary and perhaps natural love for politics—though it certainly is an unpleasant path." On another occasion she warned him, "The thorns, the thistles, and the briers, in the field of politics seldom permit the soil to produce anything, but weariness to the body, vexation to the mind, and ruin to the adventurer."

But her admirers would not let her retire in peace. She had established a reputation as a thoughtful commentator on political matters, and political leaders continued to seek out her opinion on the issues of the day: Federalists and Democratic-Republicans accused each other of betraying the public good; France threatened war with the new nation; the people's luxury and self-indulgence seemed more of a national problem than ever. Yet Mercy resisted pleas that she write publicly on such issues and mostly confined her thoughts to private letters. Responding in 1796 to a request from her friend, Congressman Elbridge Gerry, she replied, "Why do my friends call me out on politics? I wish to leave the bustle, the altercation, and the intrigues of designing men, and the pantomimes that dance in the shoals about the stage, to the sagacity and virtue of a few." She added pessimistically, "I yet hope [they] will keep the bark from sinking." Although she was too much of a political animal to relinquish politics altogether, she deliberately kept herself out of the daily fray.

At the same time that her active involvement in politics was waning, she came into her own as a writer and literary figure of note. At an age when most women were becoming grandmothers, Mercy entered a whole new phase of her career. In 1790, she published her first book. Entitled *Poems, Dramatic and Miscellaneous*, the volume brought together her recent plays, *The Sack of Rome* and *The Ladies of Castile*, along with an eclectic selection of poems, including political pieces from the revolutionary era such as "The Squabble of the Sea Nymphs," "A Poem on Primitive Simplicity," and "The Genius of America weeping the absurd Follies of the Day," which she had previously published anonymously or under a pseudonym. The compilation also contained poems dealing with more personal concerns, such as "To Fidelio, long absent on public Business," written for her husband; "To Honoria, on her Journey to Dover," composed for her friend Hannah Winthrop; and "To a

Young Gentleman, residing in France," created for her son Winslow.

The volume reflected Mercy's growing assertiveness as a woman writer. The work that opened the poetry section, "To Mrs. Montague, Author of 'Observations on the Genius and Writings of Shakespeare'" seems no accidental choice. In addressing another female author, Mercy made a public act of solidarity with other woman writers. In the poem itself, she proclaimed, "A sister's hand may wrest a female pen,/From the bold outrage of imperious men." Defending Montague—and herself—against potential critics, she added:

> Critics may frown, or mild good nature praise;
> Secure I'll walk, and placid move along,
> And heed alike their censure or their song;
> I'll take my stand by fam'd Parnassus' side,
> And for a moment feel a poet's pride.

The poem was, in effect, a declaration of personal independence, the dawn of a new, more confident Mercy Otis Warren.

Even more than the poems, the new plays revealed Mercy's changed understanding of women's role. Unlike her earlier efforts, in which female characters played only minor roles, her most recent plays included substantial parts for women. In fact, the plays' action turned on the behavior of the women, not the men. *The Sack of Rome*, written in 1785, concerned the fate of the ancient city as it was besieged by invading barbarian tribes from without and by the ruthless and evil Emperor Valentinian from within. Gaudentius, son of the slain commander of the Roman army, sought to avenge his father's death by killing his murderer, Valentinian. But doing so might well lose him the heart of Eudocia, the emperor's daughter, whom he desired to marry. It was a woman, however, who performed the key action of the entire play. In a desperate effort to restore order and to save the city from the evil emperor, Edoxia, wife of Valentinian and mother of Eudocia, opened the gates of Rome to the invading Vandals. Despite her valor, Edoxia's attempt backfired. The barbarians betrayed her. After conquering the city, the Vandals carried her daughter off to Africa, where she was to marry a barbarian prince. Edoxia herself was enslaved in golden chains and prevented from obtaining any release—even the final release offered by suicide. However conventional its structure, *The Sack of Rome* represented an important departure for Mercy. Edoxia represented a woman who actively asserted herself into the political realm. Although she was a tragic rather than a triumphant heroine, she was no passive bystander to the critical events of the day. Mercy had created a female character who openly acted on her political beliefs.

The Ladies of Castile, written in 1784, offered an even stronger vision of woman—and resolved some of the tensions latent in Mercy's earlier depictions of the female patriot. Mercy set the story in Spain, during the civil war engulfing the country in the seventeenth century. As she portrayed it, Don Velasco and his son, Conde Haro, represented the forces of tyranny, while Don Juan de Padilla and Don Francis represented the forces of virtue, the troops raised by the States of Spain. But the central action of *The Ladies of Castile* focused on the fate of two women: Donna Maria, the heroic wife of the good Padilla, and Donna Louisa, the daughter of the evil Velasco, who loved Francis, a member of the forces opposing her father.

In constructing the play, Mercy carefully set up an implicit contrast between the two women by comparing their reactions to the deaths, reported or actual, of their loved ones. Mercy depicted Louisa as a stereotype, even the caricature, of a weak woman. Upon hearing a report of her lover's death, Louisa despaired and committed suicide. When Maria heard a report of her husband's death, she chose to behave much differently. Early on, Mercy established Maria as a patriot first, a woman second. "To make atonement for the guilt of men,/. . . No fables, legends, dreams, or monkish tales,/Shake my firm purpose, or disarm my mind,/When duty calls to make my country free." In response to her husband's death, Maria became a woman of action, overcoming her feminine timidity to rouse her fellow citizens to arms. She felt "within [herself] a manly force of mind/Urging to deeds heroic and sublime,/Which but to name, one half my timid sex,/Would fall the victims of their own despair." Much as Mercy had taken over for her fallen brother James, Maria picked up where her husband had left off. (Note, too, how closely the name "Maria" resembled Mercy's own nickname, "Marcia.") In a powerful speech, Maria boldly declared her purpose to all of Spain:

> I will avenge my lord—
> Though the rough surges in loud tempests roar,
> 'Till the rude billows meet the lowering clouds—
> I never will despair, till my soul flies
> And mixes with the bold exalted shades,
> The stern brow'd spirits of the feudal lords—
> Who now bend down, and frowning from the skies,
> Chide back their dastard sons to take the field,
> Bravely to fight—to conquer or to die.

Whatever the fate of the male characters, women, Mercy implied, had a duty to carry on. She clearly sanctioned the behavior of the heroic Maria over that of the cowardly Louisa.

The Ladies of Castile also represented Mercy's belated acknowledgment of women's contribution to the American Revolution. A woman stood at the center of the main action. Far from being a suffering, passive victim, the play's heroine resoundingly affirmed the validity, even the necessity, of women to take a dynamic role in political struggles. "Virtue," as Maria remarked, "must spring from the maternal line." Mercy thus emerged from the war with a firmer sense of women's ability to control their own—and their country's—destinies. It is worth noting, however, that even in her most feminist play, Mercy portrayed a woman in politics as having "a manly force of mind." Women, as she saw it, still conceded some of their femininity when they chose to enter the political realm.

Mercy's increasing confidence in women's patriotism mirrored her growing belief in herself as a writer. Though neither *The Ladies of Castile* nor *The Sack of Rome* can be considered great plays, in the sense of making an enduring artistic contribution, they are much better works than Mercy's political satires of the 1770s. Like the earlier plays, the latter two were written in blank verse, but unlike the earlier efforts, these plays were written to be performed: they were not merely scripted dialogues. They displayed deeper character development, greater plot articulation, and a heightened sense of dramatic movement. In one of the "Gleaner" essays, Judith Sargent Murray praised Warren's "excellent tragedies that abound with the pathetic, the beautiful, and the sublime" and urged that they be performed on stage. Mercy herself tried to get them staged. In 1787 she asked John Adams, who was stationed in London, to see whether he could get *The Sack of Rome* printed and performed in England. He regretfully informed her that he could not, for "nothing American sells here." Mercy, however, did not let a setback deter her and published the plays as part of her collected works.

Poems, Dramatic and Miscellaneous brought Mercy well-deserved accolades from numerous public figures. Now that she published under her own name, she could get the credit she had long deserved. George Washington, John Adams, and others wrote to congratulate her. Alexander Hamilton remarked, "In the career of dramatic composition at least, female genius in the United States has outstripped the Male." Judith Murray sent an unsolicited letter, praising the volume for its "brilliant manifestations of Genius so conspicuously displayed therein." Mercy, she said, represented a role model for women who aspired to literary attainments. Men as well as women regarded her work as the start of an indigenous American literary tradition.

Mercy basked in the praise. In a revealing gesture, she wrote her last will and testament. She bequeathed the book's copyright to her favorite son, Winslow. The copyright was, she said, "the only thing" she "could properly call her own." As a married woman living in the eighteenth century, she did not in fact have the right to own any real property. (Some even might have disputed her legal claim to her work's copyright.) As it turned out, Winslow died before she, so the issue was never contested. Nevertheless, her act poignantly demonstrated the volume's profound significance to her.

Despite growing acclaim, Mercy's personal problems conspired to insure that she would do little new writing in the succeeding years. The deaths of Charles in 1785 and Winslow in 1791 dispirited her. "The little talent for poetry which I once possessed," she wrote to Elbridge Gerry in 1793, has been "buried in the grave[s] of my dear children." Poor health— her eyesight continued to decline and she became increasingly feeble—made writing an arduous task. After her son George died in 1800, she seemed to have even less interest in writing. Politically, however, she and James experienced a resurgence. The election of Thomas Jefferson in 1800 represented a victory for their brand of republicanism. James even roused himself from his habitual silence to congratulate the new president, heralding his election as "the triumph of Virtue over the most malignant & virulent & slandering Party that perhaps ever existed." To the Warrens' delight, Jefferson rewarded the family's loyalty with the patronage that Adams had denied them. Their son, Henry, was named customs collector for the Port of Plymouth, and James, Jr., was appointed the town's postmaster. In 1804 at the age of seventy-eight, James, Sr., also received an appointment—to the mostly honorific position as one of the presidential electors for his state.

These developments surely pleased Mercy and helped assure her that the country's future was now in the hands of those who would be more faithful to the patriots' original vision. Yet she still sounded a characteristic note of caution and skepticism. The split between Federalists and Republicans threatened the nation's very foundation and stability. "It may be that America [will] long be excused from the havoc and miseries of war:," she wrote to John Dickinson in 1807, "but what will be the consequences of our own internal divisions and party acrimony no one can calculate." Even at her most optimistic, Mercy never fully reconciled herself to the new order. She was always something of an outsider and a critic.

With Jefferson's election, Mercy finally began to feel that the time was ripe for the release of her narrative account of the American Revolution. She had begun the work in 1775, in part to pass the time during the her husband's long absences on government business. At first she intended her account to be a private reminiscence, to be shared only with family and friends. Over time, however, she began to write a more formal history with a larger audience in mind.

Mercy's *History of the Rise, Progress and Termination of the American Revolution interspersed with Biographical, Political and Moral Observations* was a monumental work. Running for three volumes, thirty-one chapters totalling 1,298 pages, the work was one of the earliest accounts of the Revolution. It was certainly the earliest history written by a woman. As unusual as it had been for a woman to write political satires during the revolutionary era, it was even more unusual for a woman to endeavor to write a work of history. By the late eighteenth century, some women, including Hannah Webster Foster and Susanna Rowson in America and Jane Austen and the Brontë sisters in England, were beginning to publish novels and short fiction. But Mercy clearly rejected that path, calling fiction "the puerile study of romance and knight errantry." History at this time, however, was written largely by and about elite white males. To write a good history, the author needed a thorough grounding in the classics, a familiarity with political theory, and an intense interest in the machinations and labyrinthine ways of power. Few women had such credentials, and even fewer had the gumption to pursue their goal—with the important exception of Catharine Macaulay, whose magisterial histories of England were respected both in America and abroad. No doubt her correspondence with Macaulay had given Mercy the inspiration and encouragement to write history herself.

Mercy began her work by drawing on personal recollections of the events she recounted. Acting as both a participant and observer, she acknowledged her privileged position, for she had been "connected by nature, friendship, and every social tie, with many of the first patriots, and most influential characters on the continents." She quickly moved beyond personal memory, however, and sought to ground her work in outside sources. Appealing to various friends and acquaintances, she requested information, documents, and descriptions of events from various public figures, including John Adams, General Benjamin Lincoln, Congressman Elbridge Gerry, and others. Much like professional historians today, she also consulted a variety of state papers and public records, including published sources such as *The Annual Register* and *The Remembrancer,* as well as works of political history and theory, such as Montesquieu's *Spirit of Laws* and Edward Gibbon's *History of the Decline and Fall of the Roman Empire.* To support her claims, she appended certain documents, including a transcript of the Articles of Confederation, the Articles of Capitulation at Yorktown, letters between principal figures such as John Dickinson and James Otis, Lord Cornwallis and Henry Clinton, and Charles Lee and Benjamin Rush, along with lists of the members of Congress and certain military instructions. Though it was by no means standard procedure at the time, she also provided footnotes identifying the sources of many of her quotations. She was a careful, exacting chronicler.

As careful as she was, Mercy was not neutral in her presentation of events. Following the dictum of Lord Bolingbroke which said, "History is philosophy teaching by examples," she had a deeper purpose guiding her study. Drawing on classical republican tropes, she sought to remind the next generation of the principles of liberty and virtue that had made success against Britain possible and republican government viable. "A concern for the welfare of society," she declared, "ought equally to glow in every human breast." She thus wrote from a well-defined point of view: as a patriot, an "old republican," a woman, and a supporter of the French Revolution. Implicitly and explicitly, she portrayed the revolutionary era as a kind of morality play that pitted virtue against vice, liberty against tyranny, and passion against reason.

Mercy's account nonetheless included everything a standard history of the revolutionary period should. She provided a detailed description of British policies and American responses to the Stamp Act, Townshend Acts, and Coercive Acts. As in her earlier plays, Thomas Hutchinson figured as the embodiment of British-led evil in the colonies. He was, she said, "the principal author of the sufferings of the unhappy Bostonians." She explored the painstaking process leading to independence, emphasizing that it was "the folly and misguided policy of the government of England [which] has dissevered the colonies from them forever." Tracing the progress of the war, she discussed the difficulties of the military campaigns and the ultimate triumph at Yorktown, where "the British themselves acknowledged, their own was fairly *outgeneralled.*" She analyzed the problems of government under the Articles of Confederation and the writing of the U.S. Constitution. Moderating her previous criticisms of the new government, she observed that "the new constitution was adopted with applause and success, and the promise and expectations of amendments flattered all classes with every advantage that could be rationally expected." Toward the end of her account, she added a brief, much less-detailed survey of the presidencies of Washington and Adams and traced the rise of party divisions. In her view, the Federalists proved themselves to be "monarchists" who had betrayed the spirit of the Revolution. True republicans such as Thomas Jefferson were the rightful heirs of the Spirit of '76.

In keeping with her grand purpose, one of Mercy's major themes was the decline in public virtue and the transformation of American manners. Like many other eighteenth-century authors, Mercy used the term "manners" not simply to refer to etiquette or social deportment, but to denote social norms or mores. In this sense, the term linked private morality and public behavior, referring as much to inner character—a person's or a nation's—as it did to outward actions. Changes in manner thus reflected changes in virtue. Invoking the commonly held four-stage theory of history, Mercy maintained that Americans had quickly passed through the stages of development. Having been "born under no feudal tenure, nurtured in the bosom of mediocrity [meaning "equality of condition"], [and] educated in the schools of freedom," Americans had demonstrated simple manners, polite tastes, and a republican willingness to sacrifice for the common good. Within only a few generations, the colonists had learned "to vie with their European ancestors in arts [and] in arms, . . . in the same space of time that most other colonies have required to pare off the ruggedness of their native ferocity, establish the rudiments of civil society, and begin the fabric of government and jurisprudence."

By the time of the Revolution, the colonists had reached the peak of their social development and, at the same time, had remained remarkably uncorrupted and virtuous. Americans were, she said, "a people uncontaminated by foreign luxury, the intricacies of foreign policies, or the theological jargon of metaphysical sceptics of foreign extract." The Revolution, in her view, changed all that. Echoing the classical republicanism of her earlier poems and plays, Mercy's *History of the American Revolution* lamented encroaching corruption and a decline in public virtue. "Avarice without frugality, and profusion without taste, were indulged," she insisted, "and soon banished the simplicity and elegance that had formerly reigned. . . . The rising generation demonstrated a thirst for the accumulation of wealth, unknown to their ancestors. A class who had not had the advantages of the best education, and who had paid little attention to the principles of the revolution, took the lead in manners." To compound the problem, organizations such as the Society of the Cincinnati[1] created the specter of hereditary titles and an American nobility—a true blight on the egalitarianism that had characterized American society, totally contrary to "that real honor which is ever the result of virtue."

Mercy traced a further threat to the civic virtue in Americans' dangerous tendency to imitate European systems and institutions. The last chapter of Mercy's work reads like a screed against "the poison of foreign influence" which, she said, spread luxury to every class, encouraged Americans to accumulate public and private debt, and incited them to become more monarchical in their government. Sounding at least as much of an isolationist as George Washington in his Farewell Address, she depicted the country as a delicate experiment in liberty that could be upset by entangling alliances with foreign nations. The United States, she said, needed to be shielded from pernicious outside forces and foreigners in their midst. "Let not the frivolity of the domestic taste of the children of Columbia, nor the examples of strangers of high or low degree, that may intermix among them, or the imposing attitude of distant nations, or the machinations of the bloody tyrants of Europe . . . rob [U.S. citizens] of their character, their morals, their religion, or their liberty." Fearing the worst, she predicted that if her fellow Americans did not heed her warnings, future historians would have to "detail the lapse, and hold up the contrast between a simple, virtuous, and free people"

---

[1]The Society of Cincinnati was formed in 1783 as a mutual aid and fraternal organization of French and American officers who had served in the Revolutionary War. George Washington, among others, was an early member. Many Americans objected to the group, in part because membership was hereditary, passed on to the eldest son.

of the revolutionary era and "a degenerate, servile race of be-
ings, corrupted by wealth, effeminated by luxury, [and] im-
poverished by licentiousness, [who had] become the *automa-
tons* of intoxicated ambition." By the end of her three volumes,
Mercy's didactic message overwhelmed her historical narrative.

Though it was not uncommon for histories at the time to
contain an explicit moral message, what made Mercy's history
most unusual was that it was written explicitly from a woman's
point of view. In her revolutionary-era plays, she had deliberately cloaked her gender from her readers, often writing from
a male point of view. By the time she published her *History of
the American Revolution*, Mercy, having gained more confidence
in herself as a woman writer, directly confronted the question
of women's relationship to the political process. Ostensibly
she affirmed a traditional view of gender roles, admitting that
"there are certain appropriate duties assigned to each sex"
and acknowledged that "it is the more peculiar province of
masculine strength. . . [to] describe the blood-stained field,
and relate the story of slaughtered armies." Yet women, she
maintained, had a stake in understanding government and
politics. Women at home could not be happy, she reasoned, if
the nation sank into despotism. Because "every domestic enjoyment" depended on "the unimpaired possession of civil and
religious liberty," she as a woman had a valid role in explaining "the great scenes that produced the revolution, and obtained independence for [the] country." Although she approached her task with a "trembling heart," she felt compelled
by higher principles—truth, justice, and candor—to pursue
her work.

Mercy's womanly perspective influenced the *History of the
American Revolution* in both obvious and subtle ways. In the
introduction, she argued that her feminine point of view informed the entire work. "The historian," she said, speaking of
herself, "has never laid aside the tenderness of the sex, or the
friend; at the same time, she has endeavoured, on all occa-

sions, that the strictest veracity should govern her heart, and
the most exact impartiality be the guide of her pen." Far from
posing as an omniscient, objective observer, she sometimes
injected herself into the narrative, reminding readers that the
writer of this particular work was a woman. "Observations on
the moral conduct of man, on religious opinion or persecu-
tions, and the motives by which mankind are actuated in their
various pursuits," she said in the midst of volume two, "will
not be censured when occasionally introduced. They are more
congenial to the taste, inclination, and sex of the writer, than
a detail of the rough and terrific scenes of war." Her perspective was different but no less meritorious than a man's.

In addition to providing specific gender markers, Mercy's
feminine concerns shaped the history in less obvious ways.
Her inclusion of certain incidents or events reflected what critic
Nina Baym has called "a gendered sense of priorities." Unlike
her male historian contemporaries, such as David Ramsay and
John Marshall, Mercy eschewed a detailed description of military strategy and battle formations in favor of discussions about
the effects of war on the civilian, especially the female, population. Describing a British attack on New Haven in July 1779,
for example, Mercy noted that ordinarily "the historian would
willingly draw a veil over the wanton outrages committed on
the wretched inhabitants left in the town, most of them of the
feebler sex." Mercy, however, felt that the enormity of these
crimes warranted their inclusion. As she explained it, a group
of American loyalists and British troops, under the leadership
of Governor Tryon, attacked the town, plundering and destroying it. She did not shrink from what happened next. The
soldiers' "barbarous abuse of the hapless females" forced the
unarmed women to fall as "sacrifices to the [men's] wanton
and riotous appetites." Male historians glossed over or ignored
the soldiers' rape and assault of women; they regarded it as a
normal and expected, if unfortunate, consequence of war. But
Mercy would not let such behavior pass without comment.

At another point, Mercy told the story of the siege of
Charleston. While affirming the courage of the male parti-

sans who held out for a month against the British, she also celebrated the patriotism of the women who participated in the struggle. The women of South Carolina submitted "to inconveniences never before felt, to hardships they had never expected; and wept in secret the miseries of their country, and their separation from their tenderest connexions." Her interest in the war's effect on women extended even to those on the other side. In two different sections, she sympathetically portrayed the hardships and suffering of two British women. One was Lady Ackland, the anxious wife of a wounded officer, and the other was Lady Asgill, the grief-stricken mother of a condemned prisoner. By including these characters, Mercy made an important statement. Gender, she suggested, superseded nationality. The suffering of wives and mothers transcended geographical boundaries to bind all women together, even in the throes of war. Mercy's *History of the Revolution* thus introduced a unique voice into the accounts of the revolutionary era.

Despite a considerable investment of time and effort in the work, Mercy did not aggressively pursue its publication. She had completed a draft of the manuscript by 1787, which she asked her friend James Winthrop to read. Although he gave a favorable verdict, pronouncing the style "perspicuous and flowing," she did not attempt to find a publisher. Lingering suspicion toward the Warrens, a political climate dominated by high Federalists, and the family's continuing personal problems made the environment seem inhospitable toward a history of the Revolution written by a former Antifederalist who happened to be a Republican woman.

Though Jefferson's election gave Mercy hope that the political climate might now be more favorable to her account, had it not been for the intervention of an old family friend, Mercy's *History of the American Revolution* might have languished indefinitely in a desk drawer in Plymouth. It was Dr. James Freeman, pastor of King's Chapel in Boston, who took it upon himself to find a printer for the volumes. Following standard practice at the time, he solicited subscribers who would purchase the tome. He personally supervised the publication process and wrote meticulous notes to Mercy describing the exact costs and procedures and asking her advice on production matters. Because she was nearly blind, she depended on her eldest son James to proofread the text and compile the index. The massive joint effort culminated in 1805 with publication of Mercy's magnum opus.

In many ways, the *History of the American Revolution* was Mercy's greatest work—the best written, most stylistically cohesive, and most intellectually ambitious production of her literary career. Not only did it convey an accurate presentation of events by someone who knew many of the principals, it also represented an Old Revolutionary's prophetic lament, the last testament of a classical republican who could not reconcile the liberalism of the new age with the values she thought had fuelled the Revolution. Yet to a significant degree Mercy's history was anachronistic by the time it was published. As a woman, she never had to translate its values into practice. As a result, her disappointment and acute sense of the country's falling away from a golden age were far sharper than most men's. Because of her distance from real-world politics, she could afford to be a more consistent classical republican than the men who had once shared her views.

For this and other reasons, the public response to Mercy's work was disappointing. In contrast to her first book, the *History* elicited no congratulations from leading figures or acclamations of her literary genius. Only one periodical, a conservative religious publication, saw fit to review it—and then only negatively. The author, said the anonymous reviewer in *The Panolpist*, drew the characters too freely, in ways "a *gentleman* would not, perhaps, have thought prudent." The work, the critic commented, was "the product of a mind that had not yet yielded to the assertion that all political attentions lay outside of the road of female life." Before the book's publication, Mercy had anticipated the possibility of criticism. "If [the history] should not escape the remarks of the critic, or the censure of party," she wrote in the introduction, "I shall feel no wound to my sensibility." But she hoped things would be different. Fellow author Judith Murray blamed the *History's* reception on the recent publication of John Marshall's *Life of Washington*, which covered the same material from a Federalist perspective, and on residual resentment of the Warrens' "political principles." Whatever her expectations, Mercy could not help but be hurt by the deafening silence and weak sales that greeted her life's work.

At least one person, however, did read her work closely, even minutely. That was her old friend and mentor, John Adams. Adams, of course, had known for many years that the history was in progress. He had encouraged Mercy to start the work and urged her to complete it—even though as early as 1780 he told her he "dread[ed]" the way she would portray him. But as relations between the two families deteriorated, contact nearly ceased. Mercy corresponded only occasionally with Abigail, rarely with John. James and John wrote not at all. Envy, too, may have also eaten away at the relationship. While the Adamses had experienced national political success and extensive travels, the Warrens had remained homebodies whose forays even into local politics were not always successful. At the time of John's election to the presidency in 1796, Mercy sent Adams a congratulatory note, but James refused—much to John's irritation. Perennially sensitive to slights herself, Mercy reported that after a hiatus of nearly twelve years, Abigail had come in 1796 to visit the Warrens. "We lately had a visit of three or four days from the vice Presidents lady," she remarked tartly, "—it was unexpected;—and whither friendly, political or accidental I know not, but she appeared very *clever.*"

But the years had taken their toll on the Adamses as well. After a divisive term, John lost the presidency to Thomas Jefferson in 1800. Licking his wounds, he retreated to the family home in Quincy, where he cultivated a prickly resentment toward those who had contributed to his defeat. Resolutely self-centered, Adams could never acknowledge that his own impe-

rious manner, disdain for the people's wishes and disregard
for their rights, as evidenced by his support of the Alien and
Sedition Acts,[2] may have played a part in the debacle. Instead,
he sought to blame others and became a bitter, frustrated man.

For many months after the publication of her *History*, Mercy
heard nothing from either John or Abigail. When John finally
did write, he unleashed a barrage of criticism that few could
sustain and even fewer could accept. In a series of ten letters
beginning on July 11, 1807, he chastised Mercy's scholarship,
impugned her personal integrity, and denigrated her family's
reputation. He dismissed her work as fiction and cast doubt
on women's ability to write history. In six replies, Mercy
mounted a spirited defense that expressed her shock, dismay,
and outrage. Through it all, she maintained her dignity and
sense of self-righteousness.

The core of their disagreement centered, not surprisingly,
on Mercy's depiction of John Adams. At the time she published her account, she acknowledged the sensitivity of her
endeavor and the possibility of offending participants in the
events described who were still alive. "The heart of the annal-
ist may sometimes be hurt by political deviations which the
pen of the historian is obliged to record," she noted by way of
introducing her remarks on Adams. Striving for honesty above
all else, she attempted to give a balanced assessment of her
old friend's strengths and weaknesses. She portrayed his private life, for example, as exemplary. He "supported," she said,
"an unimpeachable character; his habits of morality, decency
and religion, rendered him amiable in his family, and beloved

---

[2]In response to widespread criticism, especially from a partisan press, Adams
supported the passage of the Alien and Sedition laws in 1798. These laws
lengthened the amount of time necessary for naturalization (on the assump-
tion that recent immigrants tended to favor the Republican party) and provided harsh punishment for those who publicly criticized the president in
speech or writing. Though not widely enforced, the acts were widely regarded
as unconstitutional infringements on the right to free speech and a free press.

by his neighbours." As a leader, she regarded him as a figure "of penetration and ability . . . endowed with a comprehensive genius . . . actuated by the principles of integrity, by a zeal for the rights of men, and an honest indignation at the ideas of despotism." But her judgment of him as a politician was more measured—though by no means unduly harsh. "Pride of talents and much ambition," she commented, "were undoubtedly combined in the character of the president who immediately succeeded general Washington." Reflecting a common opinion at the time, Mercy maintained that after Adams had returned from England, "he was implicated by a large portion of his countrymen, as having relinquished the republican system and forgotten the principles of the American Revolution," having "discovered a partiality in favor of monarchic government." Despite such criticisms, Mercy's assessment fell well within the boundaries of what might be considered a fair and accurate evaluation of the former president. Like other leaders associated with the Federalist party, Adams had supported the creation of a strong executive with expanded powers. His *Defense of the Constitution of Government of the United States* seemed to celebrate monarchy, while his aloof behavior as president and his support for the Alien and Sedition Acts lent credence to Mercy's claims.

But Adams did not think so. Imputing the harshest, most insidious motives to Mercy, he maligned both the spirit and the letter of what she had written. Criticizing everything from debatable word choices to minor omissions to petty errors of fact, he claimed that partisan passions and personal vendettas had fatally flawed her work. He accused her of basing her judgments on insufficient information and of distorting the facts she did have. He copied out lengthy portions of official documents in order to prove his points. Finally he chastised her for ever having published the work at all, saying, "It is . . . highly reprehensible in any woman or man in the world to publish such an envenomed satire, under the grave title of a History."

Signing himself, "your injured friend," he disingenuously insisted that he addressed her "in the spirit of friendship," primarily so that Mercy could correct mistakes in the event of a future edition of her work.

Adams's specific charges suggested just how bitter and petty he had become. Attempting to rebut her portrayal of his character, he spent several pages trying to prove that he was not a man who could be characterized, as Mercy had said, as having "pride of talents." He never believed himself, he said, to be a man who "had any talents beyond mediocrity." Without the slightest sense of irony or self-contradiction, he then proclaimed in the same paragraph of the same letter that he took "great satisfaction in believing that I have done more labor, run through more and greater dangers, and made greater sacrifices than any man among my contemporaries, living or dead, in the service of my country." Turning her description of him back on her, he insisted, "If it was not 'pride,' it was presumption, 'of talent,' in a lady to write a history with so imperfect information or so little impartiality." Like the anonymous reviewer in *The Panolpist*, the fact that "a lady" had dared to write those words aggrieved him as much as anything else. Moreover, "a lady" provided an easier target for Adam's attacks than the male authors who had deprived him of the presidency.

As dismayed as she was by the assault, Mercy at first attempted to placate Adams. She was well aware, she told him, "of the difficulty and delicacy of drawing living characters." But she had written her history, "under a strong sense of the moral obligation of truth, adhering strictly to its dictates according to the best of my information, which I endeavored to draw from the purest source." No other motives—neither partisan spirit nor personal vengeance—had guided her. She reminded him of their previous friendship and of his earlier encouragement of her work. Citing a letter he had written her in 1775, she quoted him (accurately) as having said, "the faithful historian delineates characters truly, let the censure fall where it will." Obviously he had intended his words to apply only to others. Although she disputed the justice of some of his claims, she sought to restore good relations.

Adams, however, was not to be placated. As much as anything, he resented the fact that she did not assign him a larger role in history. Out of 1,298 pages, she had devoted only a total of four pages to a discussion of Adams's character and historical significance. She had acknowledged briefly (and positively) his role in the revolutionary movement, the Continental Congress, and as a diplomat abroad. But she did not provide a detailed treatment of either his or Washington's administration, considering these events to be largely outside her purview. Adams was nonetheless not satisfied. He sent pages of documentation detailing his contributions and importance. Always astute, Mercy saw through to what was really bothering him. "The resentment expressed seems principally to arise from the neglect of the writer to dilate on the honors done you by your country. . . . It was not the design of my historic work to write a panegyric on your life and character, though fully sensible of your virtues and services. You may do that yourself in some future memoir"—which he did.

Yet each of Adams's successive letters became more personal, hysterical, and vituperative than the last. Hoping to salvage their friendship, Mercy appealed to his sense of friendship, politeness, and a common past. When these failed, she took refuge in her gender. Her "sex alone," she said, "ought to have protected her from the grossness of your invectives." Nothing seemed to work. To her credit, Mercy did not shrink from a fight. When he remarked that some comment in the *History* had made him "blush" for her—as if she had made a faux pas, she denied the charge and shot back, "I advise you to . . . blush for yourself." When Adams charged her and her husband with having spread false rumors that led to his defeat for the presidency, Mercy's patience began to evaporate. "If you can infer from a history so impartially and candidly written that myself or my family have been the propagators of all the ridiculous stuff you mention previous to Mr. Jefferson's election," she told him, "I believe you are the only man in the United States that would draw such an absurd conclusion." When he volleyed yet another assault, she asserted, "Though I am fatigued with your repetition of abuse, I am not intimidated." Hoping "to be relieved from a correspondence so repugnant to [her] feelings," Mercy cooly wished her former friend well in his retirement.

Still, Adams refused to end his vituperative barrage. Broadening his attack to include Mercy's family, he claimed that "the only two offices General Warren ever held under the old Congress . . . I procured for him." He also suggested that much of Mercy's supposed animus toward him resulted from his denial of patronage for her sons. With great condescension, he told her that he surely would have appointed her husband to be customs collector for the Port of Plymouth, if he had had positions to dispense.

Outraged and exasperated, Mercy could not refrain from responding to Adams's insults of her family. Asserting her former authority, she reminded him of who he was and where he came from. She had in her possession, she said, at least twenty-five letters from John's days of "pupilage," in which Adams explicitly acknowledged his debt to James Warren. As she saw it, Adams owed his early career to her husband; James's influence had enabled John to be chosen a member of the first Congress. In those days, the younger man had taken no important step without first consulting his elder. "And is it possible," she retorted sarcastically, "that you could ever suppose that this friend to whom you once looked up with so much veneration could, in a subsequent period, ever think himself obliged, promoted, or dignified by *your* appointing him a collector for the little port of Plymouth?" In the same vein, Mercy downplayed the significance of Adams's having denied patronage to her sons. "A rough, ungentlemanly reply to that letter

was a sufficient bar," she told him, "to any subsequent applica-
tion for *your patronage*. But a circumstance of so little importance to them has never instigated the 'Warren family' to form
a junction with Burr, Hamilton, or any others in your list of
enemies, as you have insinuated, 'to turn you out of the highest office in the nation.'"

Mercy's letter of August 27, 1807, ended contact between
the Warrens and the Adamses for nearly four years. In the person of John Adams, Mercy's sense of personal victimization had
met its match. Each thought the other was out to get them. To
be fair to Adams, he undoubtedly experienced Mercy's criticisms as a personal betrayal. He had, after all, promoted her
literary career, treated her as an intellectual equal, and taken
her into his confidence. Now she seemed to be joining in the
chorus of disapproval that had denigrated his contributions to
the country and deprived him of a second term as president.
Though she claimed to be objective, she had, it was true, written a work permeated with her values as an "Old Republican"
and a long-time critic of the Federalist party. Mercy, however,
was correct to feel betrayed as well. She had publicly acknowledged her gratitude to him, having dedicated a poem ("To Mr.
—") and a play (*The Sack of Rome*) to him. Most of Adams's
charges were absurd or petty, the result of a deliberate misread-
ing of her work and a stubborn denial of her integrity as a
person and a historian. He obviously used Mercy's work as a
scapegoat for his own pent-up rage toward his detractors. Even
Elbridge Gerry, to whom Mercy appealed to arbitrate the dispute, felt that Adam's accusations lacked merit.

Despite the sadness occasioned by the rupture, in her later
years Mercy came to a new sense of inner tranquility. As she
moved into her seventies and eighties, she often found herself unable to leave home for long periods of time. In 1799,
she told Abigail Adams that she had ridden "only three miles
since my late sickness and for more than thirteen months have
set foot on the ground but once." She was quite frail and her

vision was all but gone. But her mind remained sharp and her conversation lively. She enjoyed the company of her remaining family. When Henry had married Polly Winslow on November 8, 1791, she had written a joyous letter to her new daughter-in-law. At last, Mercy said, she had someone to call "*daughter*, the endearing epithet [that] at once calls up all the feelings of the maternal heart, the sanctions, the injunctions, the anxiety, the maxims of age and experience." Less than a year later, she exulted in the birth of her first grandchild—a girl named Marcia, in honor of Mercy's favorite nickname for herself. Her granddaughter, she joked to her son, was "not tongue-tied, as that is not a deficiency incident to the family on either side." Over the years, Henry and Polly produced eight more children. Because the family lived nearby, the grandchildren could visit Mercy often, diverting and entertaining her in her old age. The other surviving son also brought her pleasure. In 1800, their eldest son left his job as a schoolteacher in a neighboring town and came home to live with his elderly parents. In the midst of her family, Mercy exuded the peace of a woman who had come to terms with her life. She was surrounded by the "little social circle" that always made her happy. "My drawing room has not been brilliant," she told a friend in 1812, "nor my parlor rounded with company, but I have had my children, my few friends, my books, and my gratitude about me, and . . . my solitary hours, which are not the least [un]pleasant—."

Despite increasing debility, Mercy welcomed her advancing years. Living in a society that revered rather than feared old age, she revelled in the perquisites to which her years entitled her. "Egotism," she wrote to little Marcia, "may be a little indulged in old age, from its long experience and want of novelty,—but in youth it is at once both impertinent and tiresome—." Self-mockingly, she told a female friend, "Aged people are apt to make the self the chief subject of converse, whether personal or epistolary. Therefore half a page of egotism is enough." In her dotage, Mercy learned to take herself a little less seriously.

But old age did bring new sorrows. She had outlived three of her five sons. Over the years, other family members and close friends passed on, beginning with the death of Hannah Winthrop in 1790, then Catharine Macaulay in 1791, her brother Joseph in 1810, and another brother, Samuel Allyne Otis, in April 1814. Eventually, she faced the ultimate grief. "The first friend of her heart" died in Plymouth on November 28, 1808. In James's memory, Mercy published an acrostic in the Boston *Independent Chronicle*, which formed her public tribute to him:

> In all the contests which his country shakes
> A patriot firm in all their griefs partakes,
> Many the virtues which adorn the man.
> Earnest his zeal to oppose the tyrant's plan
> Steady and constant to the friends he's chose
>
> Without disguise to such as are his foes
> A judgment sound, and understanding clear,
> Replete with knowledge and a heart sincere,
> Rejoicing most when most mankind are bless'd,
> Ever with generous heart aids the distress'd
> No more I'll say but time shall tell the rest.

Having been married for fifty-four eventful years, Mercy met James's departure with more equanimity than she had the untimely deaths of her sons. She realized that it was her husband's time to go—and that her time would be coming soon.

The poems she wrote late in life reflected a sense of inner calm and peaceful resignation to God's will. As she turned her mind to her eternal destiny, earthly tribulations seemed to bother her less. In "An address to the Supreme Being," she observed,

Yet for lifes blessings I'll adore
Nor of its ills complain,
For what must terminate with time
Gives little joy or pain:

For when the active thinking soul
Made to outlive the spheres,
Surveys Eternity beyond
Say what is fourscore years?

Yet the feud with Adams still rankled. She had cut off the correspondence with a demand for an apology. After four years, however, she still had not received one. Unhappy with the unresolved nature of the conflict, she broke down in November 1811 and wrote a conciliatory note to John. Delivered by their mutual friend, Massachusetts Governor Elbridge Gerry, it seemed to do the trick. Gerry reported that Adams harbored no lingering hostility toward Mercy, and out of respect for their previous friendship, wished to put the matter to rest. Contrary to Mercy's wishes, however, Adams refused to destroy his copies of the critical letters, which she felt were an embarrassment to him. In subsequent months, Abigail renewed her correspondence with Mercy, while John sent wary messages via his wife. During the summer of 1812, as the war with England was beginning, Abigail paid a personal visit to her old friend. Clearly relieved by this conciliatory gesture, Mercy wrote an exultant letter to her friend. "Blessed are the Peace makers! In that glorious band of righteous do I class my friend, Mrs. Adams."

Though Mercy and Abigail were ready to put the controversy behind them, John was not. Relations between John and Mercy remained distant. "You observed in your [letter]," she told Abigail, "'that no personal resentment or animosity exists in the mind of the person who considered himself injured.' Why should any such feelings exist in his bosom? There are none such in mine though I consider myself the injured party." Later that year, the two women exchanged tokens of friendship. Following a common practice of the time, Abigail gave Mercy a lock of hair from her and her husband's heads, which were then set into a ring. Mercy forwarded to Abigail a lock from her head, which Abigail had set into a handkerchief pin set with pearl. For Mercy, this gesture seemed to restore their friendship to its former state. "[When] I view this testimonial of their regard," she told Abigail, "I shall be daily reminded from whose head the locks were shorn; friends who have been entwined in my heart by years of endearment, which, if in any degree interrupted by incalculable circumstances, the age of us all now reminds us we have more to think of than the partial interruption of sublunary friendships."

Eventually, John, too, overcame his wounded pride. Mercy and John resumed their correspondence "in the same style of partial friendship," as Mercy put it, "which I witnessed many years ago." Exchanging a mixture of personal gossip and political news, they discussed the course of the war against Britain and the fate of mutual friends. She even called upon him to intercede on her behalf. To disprove the claims of a pretender, Mercy requested that Adams publicly acknowledge her authorship of *The Group*—which he did speedily and gallantly. Perhaps intimations of his own mortality had facilitated the reconciliation. "We have acted our parts," he told her in 1814. "The curtain will soon be drawn upon us. We must leave the future to that Providence which has protected the past."

But Adams could never entirely forgive or forget Mercy's effrontery. Even as he rehabilitated their friendship, he wrote to Elbridge Gerry, "History is not the Province of the Ladies. . . . Little Passions and Prejudices, want of Information, false Information, want of Experience, erroneous Judgment, and frequent Partiality, are among [the *History*'s] Faults." Privately, he felt he had made a mistake by suggesting that Mercy write the work. He was not prepared, as he once advised her, to "let the Censure fall where it will." Toward the end of her life, however, Mercy needed no one's permission—least of all a man's—to write whatever she chose. She realized that politics was as much a woman's territory as it was a man's. She had indeed refused to yield, as *The Panolpist*'s critic said, "to the assertion that all political attentions lay out of the road of female life."

* * *

Mercy Otis Warren's long life ended as much of it had been spent—in the midst of a war. During the War of 1812, the British raided the country's northeastern coast, stripping and burning all in their path. "We are hourly expecting [that] the depredations of the British will break upon us," she reported to her sister-in-law in June 1814. "Ruin threatens us in plain language." She met the assault with calm. "I would not have you think [that] I am alarmed by womanish fear or the madness of old age. I am not." As usual, she trusted in Providence to come to her aid, and was spared. The following autumn, she contracted a sudden illness. Early in the morning of October 19, 1814, at the age of eighty-six, the great drama of her life came to a close.

The Line beyond her Sex

In her 1929 classic, *A Room of One's Own*, novelist and social critic Virginia Woolf speculated on why women, until very recently, had not produced great literary works. She argued that even if Shakespeare had had an equally talented sister, she never would have written great plays. As a woman, Shakespeare's sister would not have had access to the education, the range of experiences, the leisure, or the social and financial support that would have allowed her to express herself through literary means. "That woman," she concluded, "who was born with a gift of poetry in the sixteenth century, was an unhappy woman, a woman at strife against herself. All the conditions of her life, all her own instincts, were hostile to the state of mind which is needed to set free whatever is in the brain."

For Mercy Otis Warren, this was not the case. As the sister of James Otis, she received a classical education similar to that of her brother. As the daughter of Colonel James Otis, she obtained instruction in the complex customs of the political world. As the wife of James Warren, she had the benefit of a loving husband who supported his wife's unconventional abilities. Good family friends, such as John Adams, encouraged and facilitated the expression of her literary talents, even when they impinged on traditionally male areas, such as politics. These special dispensations enabled her to escape the "narrow bounds" of female life and to fulfill her potential as an author, historian, and political thinker. Unlike most women of the late eighteenth century, Warren lived in an environment that allowed her to "set free" whatever was in her brain.

As a result, she left behind a rich legacy. Having borne five sons, her line produced a nephew, Harrison Gray Otis, who became a famous Federalist politician, and a great-grandson, Charles Warren, who became a noted legal historian. As important as she saw her role as mother, she also found time to make a significant contribution to the revolutionary movement. Her political plays, satires, and poetry helped to generate a spirit of resistance to British tyranny and sustain a belief in the importance of civic virtue in republican government. During the debate over the ratification of the U.S. Constitution, she published an incisive critique that helped stimulate popular sentiment in favor of a Bill of Rights. Her *History of the American Revolution*, published in 1805, was one of the earliest and most accurate histories of the independence movement. Beyond its historical soundness, the work conveyed a sense of grandeur, intellectual ambitiousness, and moral integrity that impresses even today. Through it, Warren found the most suitable vehicle for her literary talents and the fullest expression of her political temperament. She also became the first female American historian.

On the basis of her behavior, one might, by contemporary standards, consider Warren a feminist. But she herself did not subscribe to such beliefs. She accepted the subordination of women to men, believed in separate spheres for each sex, and supported the division of occupations based on gender. She never advocated a public role for women, either in the professions or in politics. Women, she suggested should exercise influence through "the soft whisper of private friendship" rather than in public forums. Thus while she transcended the traditional boundaries of womanhood in her private life, she felt unwilling or unable to challenge those limits publicly. Over time, Warren did become more insistent about her right to discuss political issues, in print as well as in private. Women, she concluded, had as much a stake in government and politics as the men who actually ran things. When John Adams challenged the validity of her *History*, Mercy told him in no uncertain terms that she would neither be intimidated into silence nor modify her assertions. Her work would stand or fall on its own merits, regardless of the author's sex.

While her positions may seem paradoxical, if not self-contradictory to us today, Mercy found a way to live with the tension. Unlike her British contemporary, Mary Wollstonecraft, and her younger American counterpart, Judith Sargent Murray, Warren could not conceive of women being educated for a profession or participating more directly in the political process. She worked within the existing gender roles rather than challenging them directly, affirming patriarchy at the same time she circumvented its most confining limitations. Perhaps because she was able to find a personal accommodation for herself, she felt no urgency in demanding a comprehensive redefinition of women's role. Yet hers was an uneasy resolution. Though she was a talented, independent woman, she lacked a coherent ideology to explain or justify her excursions into politics. As a result, she remained vulnerable to criticism for having transgressed the established gender norms, having approached, as she once had told Adams, so near "the verge of any thing so far beyond the line of my sex." Men granted her their permission to trespass onto their territory; they could just as easily withdraw it—as Adams's subsequent attack and *The Panolpist*'s critical review of her *History* so vividly demonstrated. Mercy's lack of a feminist consciousness had other consequences as well. She failed to provide a viable role model for other women. Although she represented a stellar example of what an unusually gifted female could do when given the proper encouragement and opportunity, she was so exceptional in so many ways that she produced few literary successors and no spiritual heirs—Judith Murray notwithstanding. Her dilemma was to be a feminist without feminism.

Yet Warren's basic conservatism should not surprise us. As historians such as Linda Kerber and Mary Beth Norton have shown, the American Revolution produced only limited effects on women's status. In their roles as wives and mothers, women were, for the first time, seen to make a crucial but indirect contribution to the success of the republic. A few states loosened the strictures on divorce and broadened married women's property rights. New Jersey briefly granted women the right to vote, beginning in 1776. In the long run, however, the Revolution's most important effect on women was to expand the number, kind, and quality of educational opportunities available to them. In the decades following independence, the rate of female literacy surged, with all that that implied for women's professional and social status. It also altered their political ideas. As more and more women learned to read, they could more readily participate in the political debates of the day, both within their homes and in the semipublic arenas known as benevolent organizations.

Despite these changes, in practice the Revolution did little to alter the position of women. There were no collective protests for women's rights, no organizations created to expand their privileges. When the New Jersey assembly stripped women of their right to vote in 1807, no one—not even the women of New Jersey themselves—objected. Few writers explicitly considered the question of women's rights. In fact, many authors, both men and women alike, boasted that women in America already enjoyed a higher standing than females in any other country. "Under the mild influence of Christianity and the easy subsistence to be procured in our republican states," proclaimed Samuel L. Mitchill in 1804, "the condition of women is undoubtedly preferable to that of their sex in any part of the globe. They ought to know that Fredonia [the United States] is a woman's terrestrial Paradise. Here they are the rational companions of men, not their playthings or slaves." Or as Hannah Foster put it in 1798, "Thrice blessed are we, the happy daughters of this land of liberty, where the female mind is unshackled by the restraints of tyrannical custom, which in many other regions confines the exertions of genius to the usurped powers of lordly men! Here, virtue, merit, and abilities are properly estimated under whatever form they appear." In this context, Warren's refusal to question the existing gender structure reflected less her own intransigence on the issue and more a larger social reluctance to challenge the status quo.

Mercy's inability to conceive of a direct political role for women also reveals why feminism did not and, given the historical circumstances, could not emerge in the wake of the American Revolution. Except for a brief period during the war, Warren had no sense of gender identity and little sense of solidarity with other women. As historian Nancy Cott has explained it in *The Bonds of Womanhood*, women did not begin to identify themselves as a distinct group until the early decades of the nineteenth century. Once larger numbers of women began to work together in various voluntary societies and benevolent organizations, they came to see how much they had in common with other women. By participating in the activities of a Bible society, the temperance movement, or an anti-slavery organization, women gained a new sense of their common bonds as well as insight into their common constraints. Gender identity and a sense of group consciousness formed the necessary preconditions for women's emerging sense of entitlement to certain political rights and legal privileges, a sense that would gain formal expression for the first time at the Seneca Falls Convention of 1848. Mercy did not have the benefit of such experiences.

A comparison of Warren with a female writer of a slightly later generation helps us measure the distance that some women would traverse within a very short time. Harriet

Beecher Stowe was the author of *Uncle Tom's Cabin*, a novel that perhaps more than any other single work helped crystallize antislavery sentiment throughout the North. Her father, Lyman Beecher, was a famous Congregationalist minister and a leader of the religious upheaval known as the Second Great Awakening. Yet Harriet as well as some of her siblings gained prominence in their own right. Her sister, Catharine, published popular works on domestic economy and agitated against slavery. Harriet chose a more literary route to fame. Like Mercy, Harriet tried to balance the demands of motherhood with those of writing for publication. She bore three children in her first two years of marriage, including a set of twins. But unlike Mercy, Harriet was unabashedly assertive about the purpose and significance of her writing. In 1838, she described her attitude to her friend, Mary Dutton:

> I have about three hours per day in writing, & if you see my name coming out everywhere—you may be sure of one thing, that *I do it for the pay*. I have determined not to be a mere domestic slave—without even the leisure to *excel* in my duties. I mean to have money enough to have my house kept in the best manner & yet to have time for reflection & that preparation for the education of my children which every mother needs. I have every prospect of succeeding in this plan.

Confident of her talents, Harriet would publish political works—novels to be sure—under her own name—and expect to be paid. She wanted a proper home, but she would use her earnings to pay others to keep house for her. Determined not to be "a mere domestic slave," she would devote herself to her two top priorities, her writing and her children. Of course, Stowe, like the women who gathered at Seneca Falls, represented only a small elite. In the antebellum era, most American women neither wanted political rights nor demanded an expansion of their occupational opportunities. Nevertheless, Stowe's life demonstrates that within a few short decades certain American women had come far from Mercy's position.

They regarded politics not as a betrayal of their femininity, but an affirmation of it. Rather than trespassing onto men's territory, they believed they were extending women's realm.

To point out Warren's limitations or the ways in which she was a product of her times does not lessen the magnitude of her accomplishments. The fact that Mercy overcame enormous social strictures to become a published author and respected political thinker remains an enduring and impressive achievement. Perhaps her most important legacy, however, was the way in which she endowed individual women with a new sense of their own dignity and competence. "You seem hurt by the general aspersions so often thrown on the Understanding of ours by the Illiberal Part of the other Sex," she wrote to a young woman.

> The pride you feel . . . is a kind of conscious dignity that ought rather to be cherish'd, for while we own the appointed subordination (perhaps for the sake of order in families) let us by no means acknowledge such an inferiority as would check the ardour of our endeavours, to equal in all mental accomplishments the most masculine heights, that when these temporary distinctions subside we may be equally qualified to taste the full draughts of knowledge & happiness prepared for the upright of every nation & sex, when virtue alone will be the test of rank.

Her view of a gender-neutral world is a vision to which many would assent even today.

BIBLIOGRAPHICAL ESSAY

Primary Sources

Mercy Otis Warren's own writings constitute the principal sources for this study. Fortunately, most of these sources are readily available, either in published or microfilm form. The Massachusetts Historical Society in Boston holds the archival originals of the Mercy Warren Papers, which include the Letterbook and Miscellaneous letters, respectively on Reel One and Two of the Microfilm edition. Letters written by Mercy before the 1770s (by which time she was a mature woman in her forties) are rare. She apparently wrote many letters to her brother James, but he burned all of his correspondence after going mad. As a result, our knowledge of her early life is extremely limited. Although the Letterbook contains the most complete run of Mercy's letters in existence, the editors of the *Adams Family Correspondence* warn that the Letterbook represents a series of transcriptions that may not always be faithful reproductions of Warren's actual letters (I: 93, 94n.1). In many cases, however, they are the only copies of the letters known to exist. Other published collections of letters supplement the Mercy Warren Papers, including the *Warren-Adams Letters, Being chiefly a correspondence among John Adams, Samuel Adams, and James Warren* (Boston: The Massachusetts Historical Society, 1917), 2 vols., and L. H. Butterfield, ed., *Adams Family Correspondence* (Cambridge, Mass.: Harvard University Press, 1963–). The controversy between Mercy and John Adams is preserved in painful detail in Charles Francis Adams, ed., *Correspondence between John Adams and Mercy Warren* (New York: Arno Press, 1972), which is a reprint of the original publication found in the *Collections of the Massachusetts Historical Society*, 5th ser. (Boston, 1878), 317–491. Certain letters between Mercy and her favorite son Winslow are extensively quoted in Charles Warren, "A Young American's Adventures in England and France During the Revolutionary War," *Proceedings*, October 1932–May 1936, Massachusetts Historical Society 65 (1940), 234–67. *A Study in Dissent: The Warren-Gerry Correspondence, 1776–1792*, edited by C. Harvey Gardiner (Carbondale, Ill.: Southern Illinois University Press, 1968) reprints letters between the Warrens and Elbridge Gerry, who became Mercy's primary male correspondent after the breech with John Adams in the 1780s.

Many of Warren's own publications have been reprinted for the convenience of students and scholars. Benjamin Franklin V's edition of *The Plays and Poems of Mercy Otis Warren* (Delmar, N.Y.: Scholars' Facsimiles & Reprints, 1980) incorporates the revolutionary-era plays, *The Adulateur, The Defeat*, and *The Group*, as well as *Poems, Dramatic and Miscellaneous*, Mercy's 1790 book that also includes the plays, *The Sack of Rome* and *The Ladies of Castile*, and various poems on political and personal subjects. Poems that Mercy did not publish in her lifetime have been published by Edmund M. Hayes in "The Private Poems of Mercy Otis Warren," *The New England Quarterly* 54 (June 1981), 199–224. Mercy's letter to Winslow criticizing Lord Chesterfield appears in Edward M. Hayes, "Mercy Otis Warren versus Lord Chesterfield," *The William & Mary Quarterly* 40 (October 1983), 616–21. Her critique of the U.S. Constitution, "Observations on the New Constitution, and on the Federal and State Conventions," by "A Columbian Patriot" (Boston 1788), once attributed to Elbridge Gerry but now definitively shown to be Mercy's, is most recently available in *The Complete Anti-Federalist*, ed., with Commentary and Notes by Herbert J. Strong (Chicago: University of Chicago Press, 1981), 4: 270–87. Her 1805 masterpiece, *History of the Rise, Progress and Termination of the American Revolution interspersed*

with Biographical, Political and Moral Observations, has been edited by Lester H. Cohen and republished in 1988 by the Liberty Press of Indianapolis. For the convenience of scholars,
complete references to all the quotations I have cited have
been deposited at the Massachusetts Historical Society in Boston.

Secondary Sources

Despite her historical significance, relatively few historians have
attempted to grapple with Mercy Otis Warren's life in a sys-
tematic fashion. Alice Brown's *Mercy Warren* (New York: Charles
Scribner's Sons, 1968 [originally published in 1896]) was the
first published, full-length biography of Warren. Although it
has the limitations of the "great woman" genre of history, it
does contain some useful factual information. Katharine S.
Anthony's treatment, *First Lady of the Revolution: The Life of Mercy
Otis Warren* (New York: Doubleday and Co., Inc., 1958), is a
straight-forward chronological narrative, but it is well written,
lively, and thorough. More scholarly is Jean Fritz's *Cast for a
Revolution: Some American Friends and Enemies, 1728–1814* (Boston: Houghton-Mifflin Co., 1972), which not only discusses
Mercy's life but the activities of the whole circle around her,
including James Warren, James Otis, and John Adams. Two
dissertations provide detailed accounts of the events in Mercy's
life. Mary Elizabeth Regan's "Pundit and Prophet of the Old
Republic: The Life and Times of Mercy Otis Warren, 1728–
1814," Ph.D. diss., University of California, Berkeley, 1984, is
stronger on description than analysis, while Maud M.
Hutcheson's, "Mercy Warren: A Study of Her Life and Works,"
Ph.D. diss., American University, 1951, makes a good effort to
contextualize the writings, though the historiography is by now
quite dated. Hutcheson's article, "Mercy Warren, 1728–1814,"
The William & Mary Quarterly 10 (July 1953), 378–402, remains
one of the best short introductions to Warren's life and writings. John J. Waters, Jr., pays little attention to the female Otises

in *The Otis Family in Provincial and Revolutionary Massachusetts* (Chapel Hill: University of North Carolina Press, 1968); nevertheless, his study of the family provides an essential understanding of Mercy's background. Lester Cohen has made an impressive effort to locate Warren's work in light of recent historiographical trends. Although he focuses on her letters and *History of the American Revolution* at the expense of considering her poems and plays, his "Mercy Otis Warren: The Politics of Language and the Aesthetics of Self," *American Quarterly* 35 (1983), 481–98, and "Explaining the Revolution: Ideology and Ethics in Mercy Otis Warren's Historical Theory," *William & Mary Quarterly* 37 (April 1980), 200–18, do an excellent job of showing the influence of classical republicanism and gender on her thinking. Two outstanding works on early American women have made the present analysis of Mercy's life possible: Linda K. Kerber's *Women of the Republic: Intellect & Ideology in Revolutionary America* (New York: W.W. Norton & Co., 1980) and Mary Beth Norton's *Liberty's Daughters: The Revolutionary Experience of American Women, 1750–1800* (Boston: Little-Brown and Co., 1980). Although neither work considers Warren in depth, both mention her life in the context of other revolutionary-era women.

Chapter One: The First Friends of Her Heart

In the last three decades, historians studying the social history of colonial Massachusetts have revolutionized the field. This recent work informs my analysis of Mercy's childhood and young adulthood. Waters's *Otis Family in Provincial and Revolutionary Massachusetts* provides a superb model of a generational study, which gives insight into the larger forces that shaped the lives of the Otises. David Hackett Fischer's *Albion's Seed: Four British Folkways in America* (New York: Oxford University Press, 1989), Gary B. Nash's *Urban Crucible: The Northern Seaports and the Origins of the American Revolution* (Cambridge, Mass.: Harvard University Press, 1979), Edward M. Cook's *Fathers of the Towns: Leadership and Community Structure in Eighteenth-Century New England* (Baltimore: The Johns Hopkins University Press, 1976), and Michael Zuckerman's *Peaceable Kingdoms: New England Towns in the Eighteenth Century* (New York: Alfred A. Knopf, 1970) offer crucial information on the political changes in the colony during the late colonial era. Some older works present interesting anecdotes about early Massachusetts social customs, especially Alice Morse Earle, *Customs and Fashions in Old New England* (New York: Charles Scribner's Sons, 1902) and Samuel Eliot Morison, *Three Centuries of Harvard, 1639–1936* (Cambridge, Mass.: Harvard University Press, 1946). Although Mercy's brother James is a fascinating figure in his own right, there is no recent, full-length biography, partly because he destroyed his private correspondence. The standard older treatment is William Tudor, *The Life of James Otis of Massachusetts: Containing also, Notices of Some Contemporary Characters and Events from the Year 1760 to 1775* (Boston: Wells and Lilly, 1823). John J. Waters presents an interesting sketch of Otis in "James Otis, Jr.: An Ambivalent Revolutionary," *History of Childhood Quarterly* 1 (Summer 1973), 142–50. Studies of women and the family have greatly expanded our understanding of the contours of women's experience in colonial Massachusetts. Philip Greven's *The Protestant Temperament: Patterns of Child-Rearing, Religious Experience, and the Self in Early America* (New York: Alfred A. Knopf, 1977) provides a stimulating analysis that links the psychological, religious, and political dimensions of early American life and suggests clues to Mercy's development. Other important studies that undergird my analysis of Warren's early life include: Carole Shammas, "The Domestic Environment in Early Modern England and America," *Journal of Social History* 14 (Fall 1980), 3–24; Daniel Scott Smith, "Parental Power and Marriage Patterns: An Analysis of Historical Trends in Hingham, Massachusetts," *Journal of Marriage and the Family* 35 (August 1973), 419–28; Kenneth A. Lockridge, *Literacy in Colonial New England: An Enquiry into the Social Context of Literacy in the Early Modern West* (New York: W.W. Norton

& Co., Inc., 1974); Laurel Thatcher Ulrich, "Martha Ballard and Her Girls: Women's Work in Eighteenth-Century Maine," in *Work and Labor in Early America*, edited by Stephen Innes (Chapel Hill: University of North Carolina Press, 1988), 70–105. Cathy N. Davidson, "The Life and Times of 'Charlotte Temple': The Biography of a Book," 157–79, and E. Jennifer Monaghan, "Literacy Instruction and Gender in Colonial New England," 53–80, are both included in *Reading in America: Literature and Social History*, edited by Cathy N. Davidson (Baltimore: The Johns Hopkins University Press, 1989).

Chapter Two: Politics as a Family Affair

As in the previous chapter, Waters's *Otis Family in Provincial and Revolutionary Massachusetts* presents background material essential for explaining the context in which Mercy grew to political maturity. Other works that shaped my understanding of the political situation in late colonial Massachusetts include Richard L. Bushman's *King and People in Provincial Massachusetts* (Chapel Hill: University of North Carolina Press, 1985); Bernard Bailyn's brilliant study of Thomas Hutchinson, *The Ordeal of Thomas Hutchinson* (Cambridge, Mass.: Harvard University Press, 1974); Edmund S. and Helen M. Morgan's classic work, *The Stamp Act Crisis: Prologue to Revolution* (New York: Macmillian Publishing Co., Inc., 1953); and Pauline Maier's superb analysis of the resistance movement contained in *From Resistance to Revolution: Colonial radicals and the development of American opposition to Britain, 1765–1776* (New York: Random House, 1972). For good discussions of James Otis's ideas, see John J. Waters and John A. Schutz, "Patterns of Massachusetts Colonial Politics: The Writs of Assistance and the Rivalry between the Otis and Hutchinson Families," *The William & Mary Quarterly* 24 (October 1967), 543–67, and James R. Ferguson, "Reason in Madness: The Political Thought of James Otis," *The William & Mary Quarterly* 36 (April 1979), 194–214. Works by social historians studying early American women help fill out the portrait of a woman's daily life and the experience of mothering in the eighteenth century. These works include three by Laurel Thatcher Ulrich, *Good Wives: Image and Reality in the Lives of Women in Northern New England, 1650–1750* (New York: Oxford University Press, 1980), *A Midwife's Tale: The Life of Martha Ballard Based on Her Diary, 1785–1812* (New York, Vintage Books, 1990), and "'The Living Mother of a Child': Midwifery and Mortality in Post-Revolutionary New England," *The William & Mary Quarterly* 46 (January 1989), 27–48. Also noteworthy is Ross S. Beales's "Nursing and Weaning in an Eighteenth-Century New England Household," *Families and Children*, The Dublin Seminar for New England Folklife: Annual Proceedings 1985 (Boston: Boston University, 1985), 48–93. Kerber's *Women of the Republic* provides important information about the intellectual context of attitudes toward women in the eighteenth century as does Jacqueline S. Reiner, "Rearing the Republican Child: Attitudes and Practices in Post-Revolutionary Philadelphia," *The William & Mary Quarterly* 39 (January 1982), 150–63; Rosemarie Zagarri, "Morals, Manners, and the Republican Mother," *American Quarterly* 44 (June 1992), 26–43; and Jay Fliegelman, *Prodigals and Pilgrims: The American Revolution against Patriarchal Authority, 1750–1800* (Cambridge: Cambridge University Press, 1982).

Chapter Three: Her Pen as a Sword

Works that treat the growth of opposition to the Crown in Massachusetts include Bernard Bailyn, *The Ideological Origins of the American Revolution* (Cambridge, Mass.: Harvard University Press, 1967); Gordon S. Wood, *The Radicalism of the American Revolution* (New York: Alfred A. Knopf, 1991); Richard D. Brown, *Revolutionary Politics in Massachusetts: The Boston Committee of Correspondence and the Towns, 1772–1774* (Cambridge, Mass.: Harvard University Press, 1970); and Pauline Maier's *From Resistance to Revolution*. On the antagonism between

Hutchinson and the Otis family, see Waters and Schutz, "Patterns of Massachusetts Colonial Politics: The Writs of Assistance and the Rivalry between the Otis and Hutchinson Families," and Bailyn, *The Ordeal of Thomas Hutchinson*. There is a fairly extensive journal literature analyzing Warren's revolutionary-era plays, mostly from a literary perspective. Works most helpful to my analysis include Gerald Weales, "*The Adulateur* and How it Grew," *The Library Chronicle of the Friends of the University of Pennsylvania Library* 43 (1979), 103–33; Jean B. Kern, "Mercy Otis Warren: Dramatist of the American Revolution," *Curtain Calls: British and American Women and the Theater, 1660–1820* (Athens, Ohio: Ohio University Press, 1991), 247–59; Joan Hoff Wilson and Sharon L. Bollinger, "Mercy Otis Warren: Playwright, Poet, and Historian of the American Revolution (1728–1814)," in *Female Scholars: A Tradition of Learned Women Before 1800,* edited by J. R. Brink (Montreal: Eden Press, 1980), 161–82. Much disagreement exists about whether Mercy wrote two other plays, *The Blockheads* and *The Motley Assembly*. While Alice Brown, Maud Hutcheson, Lester Cohen, and others do not attribute these plays to her, Mary Coit Tyler, Paul Leicester Ford, Mary Regan, and John J. Teunissen (in "Blockheadism and the Propaganda Plays of the American Revolution" *Early American Literature* 7 (Fall 1972), 148–62) do assign them to her. For reasons explained in the text, I am firmly convinced Mercy did not author these works.

Chapter Four: War Widows

The standard works on women in the revolutionary era are Norton's *Liberty Daughters* and Kerber's *Women of the Republic*. Other more specialized treatments of women's experiences include Joy Day Buel and Richard Buel, *The Way of Duty: A Woman and Her Family in Revolutionary America* (New York: W.W. Norton & Co., 1984); Alfred F. Young, "The Women of Boston: 'Persons of Consequence' in the Making of the American

Revolution, 1756–76," in *Women & Politics in the Age of the Democratic Revolution*, edited by Harriet B. Applewhite and Darline G. Levy (Ann Arbor: University of Michigan Press, 1990), 181–226; and Jan Lewis, "The Republican Wife: Virtue and Seduction in the Early Republic," *The William & Mary Quarterly* 44 (Oct. 1987), 689–721. On Abigail Adams, see a fine analysis grounded in a thorough, but critical, reading of feminist literature in Edith B. Gelles's *Portia: The World of Abigail Adams* (Bloomington: Indiana University Press, 1992). For a more conventional biography, see Lynne Withey's *Dearest Friend: A Life of Abigail Adams* (New York: The Free Press, 1981).

Chapter Five: An Old Republican

Gordon Wood's *The Creation of the American Republic, 1776–1787* (New York: W.W. Norton, 1969) represents the classic discussion of political ideas during the revolutionary and constitutional eras. On changing concepts of virtue, see Myron F. Wehjte, "The Ideal of Virtue in Post-Revolutionary Boston," *Historical Journal of Massachusetts* 17 (Winter 1989), 67–83; Lance Banning, "Some Second Thoughts on Virtue and the Course of Revolutionary Thinking," in *Conceptual Change and the Constitution*, edited by Terence Bell and John Pocock (Lawrence, Kans.: University of Kansas Press, 1988), 194–212; and Ruth H. Bloch, "The Gendered Meanings of Virtue in Revolutionary America," *Signs* 13 (Autumn 1987), 37–68. Stephen E. Patterson, *Political Parties in Revolutionary Massachusetts* (Madison: University of Wisconsin Press, 1973) and Van Beck Hall, *Politics Without Parties: Massachusetts, 1780–1791* (Pittsburgh: University of Pittsburgh Press, 1972) discuss the intricacies of Massachusetts state politics, while David P. Szatmary's *Shays' Rebellion: The Making of and Agrarian Insurrection* (Amherst: University of Massachusetts Press, 1980) and *In Debt to Shays: The Bicentennial of an Agrarian Rebellion*, edited by Robert A. Gross (Charlottesville: University Press of Virginia,

1993) give particular attention to Shays's Rebellion. Excellent analyses of the Antifederalist position during the debate over ratification of the U.S. Constitution include Pauline Maier, *The Old Revolutionaries: Political Lives in the Age of Samuel Adams* (New York: W.W. Norton & Co., 1976) and Herbert Storing, *What the Anti-Federalists Were For* (Chicago: University of Chicago Press, 1981).

Chapter Six: "History is not the Province of the Ladies"

On the emergence of political parties in the United States, Richard Hofstadter's *The Idea of the Party System: The Rise of Legitimate Opposition in the United States, 1780–1840* (Berkeley, Calif.: University of California Press, 1968) is still the standard work. For the Federalists, see James M. Banner, *To the Hartford Convention: The Federalists and the Origins of Party Politics in Massachusetts, 1789–1815* (New York: Alfred A. Knopf, 1970); David Hackett Fischer, *The Revolution of American Conservatism: The Federalist Party in the Era of Jeffersonian Democracy* (New York: Harper & Row, 1965); Stanley Elkins and Eric McKitrick, *The Age of Federalism: The Early American Republic, 1788–1800* (New York: Oxford University Press, 1993); and on the Democratic-Republicans, see Joyce Appleby, *Capitalism and a New Social Order: The Republican Vision of the 1790s* (New York: New York University Press, 1984); Drew McCoy, *The Elusive Republic: Political Economy in Jeffersonian America* (Chapel Hill: University of North Carolina Press, 1980); and Lance Banning, *The Jeffersonian Persuasion: Evolution of a Party Ideology* (Ithaca, N.Y.: Cornell University Press, 1978). There are several stimulating treatments of Warren's *History of the American Revolution.* Among the most provocative are Lester Cohen's article in the *William & Mary Quarterly*, mentioned above, and his expanded discussion in *The Revolutionary Histories: Contemporary Narratives of the American Revolution* (Ithaca, N.Y.: Cornell University Press,

1980). Nina Baym's "Mercy Otis Warren's Gendered Melodrama of Revolution," *The South Atlantic Quarterly* 90 (Summer 1991), 531–54, gives a fascinating literary analysis of the work. Wilson and Bollinger's "Mercy Otis Warren: Playwright, Poet, and Historian of the American Revolution (1728–1814)," mentioned above, is a more straightforward summary, but puts the *History* in the context of Mercy's other works. One of the few analyses of *The Ladies of Castile* is contained in Kerber's *Women of the Republic,* 269–71. A good biography of Catharine Macaulay, Mercy's role model as a historian, is Bridget Hill's *The Republican Virago: The Life and Times of Catharine Macaulay, Historian* (Oxford: Clarendon Press, 1992). On the later John Adams, see Joseph J. Ellis's wonderful biography, *Passionate Sage: The Character and Legacy of John Adams* (New York: W.W. Norton, 1993).

Conclusion: The Line beyond Her Sex

Once again, Kerber's *Women of the Republic* and Norton's *Liberty's Daughters* represent the starting point for understanding the full significance of Warren's life. Nancy F. Cott's *Bonds of Womanhood: 'Woman's Sphere' in New England, 1780–1835* (New Haven: Yale University Press, 1977) explains the emergence of a subsequent generation of women who differed from Mercy's own cohort. Works that provide a basis of comparison between Mercy's life and that of other literary women include William St Clair on Mary Wollstonecraft in *The Godwins and the Shelleys: The Biography of a Family* (London: Faber and Faber, 1989) and Joan D. Hedrick's *Harriet Beecher Stowe: A Life* (New York: Oxford University Press, 1994). Judith Sargent Murray's major work has recently been reprinted as *The Gleaner,* edited with an introductory essay by Nina Baym (Schenectady, N.Y.: Union College Press, 1992). For discussions of the brief emergence of women's suffrage in the post-revolutionary era, see Edmund Raymond Turner, "Women's Suffrage in New Jersey:

1790–1807," *Smith College Studies in History* 1 (July 1916), 165–87 and Judith Apter Klinghoffer and Lois Elkis, "'The Petticoat Electors': Women's Suffrage in New Jersey, 1776–1807," *Journal of the Early Republic* 12 (Summer 1992), 159–93.

INDEX

(Mercy Otis Warren has been abbreviated to MOW.)

A Woman's Dilemma: Mercy Otis Warren and the American Revolution
Copy editor, Andrew J. Davidson
Production editor, Lucy Herz
Cartographer, Alison Hanham
Typesetter, Robin M. Stearns
Printer, McNaughton & Gunn

About the author: Rosemarie Zagarri is Associate Professor of History at George Mason University, Fairfax, Virginia. She received her Ph.D. from Yale University in 1984 and is the author of *The Politics of Size: Representation in the United States, 1776–1850* (1987) and the editor of *David Humphreys' "Life of General Washington,"* with *George Washington's "Remarks"* (1991).